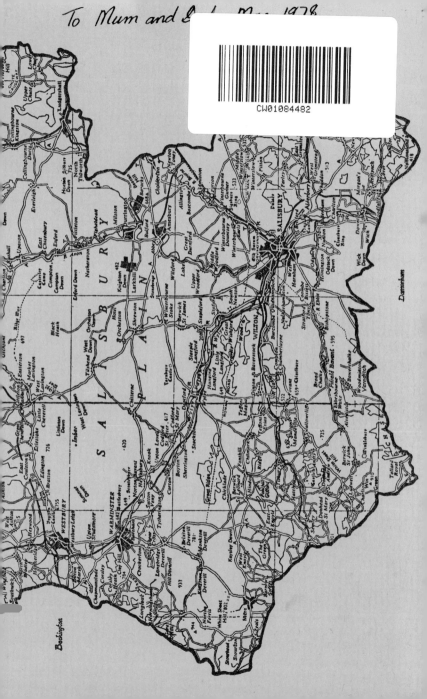

WILTSHIRE FOLKLORE

Also by Kathleen Wiltshire

GHOSTS AND LEGENDS OF THE WILTSHIRE
COUNTRYSIDE

WILTSHIRE FOLKLORE

KATHLEEN WILTSHIRE

EDITED BY PATRICIA M. C. CARROTT

Illustrated by Hilary Williams

COMPTON RUSSELL

First published in Great Britain 1975
by Compton Russell Ltd.,
Compton Chamberlayne, Salisbury, Wiltshire
and printed there by
The Compton Press Ltd

ISBN 0 85955 016 8

for
MARNEY, ANNE AND PETER
some of their county's lore

Contents

I

WITCHES

*'The cult of the Witch is as old as humanity ...
as flourishing today as in the fifteenth century,
and as firmly believed.'*
                    J. W. BRODIE-INNES

In grandmother's young days witches were looked upon
as quite usual members of society, and she used to tell us
of one who lived in her village who used to cure minor
illnesses such as sore eyes using 'fasting spittle'. This was,
of course, a village 'wise woman'. Tales about them have
been long established in Wiltshire; indeed, John Aubrey
wrote, 'In these well clayey parts there have ever been
reputed witches.' My grandmother used to say that a sure

way to keep a witch outside your home was to hang a garland of holly and bay outside the front door at Christmas :
the witch would remain there, counting the holly berries –
indefinitely, presumably, since witches only count up to
four before starting again at one.

Scattered around the county are many churches whose
fonts in the old days were locked against witches, who
otherwise would have stolen the consecrated water to use
in their noxious arts. I myself have discovered at least
fifteen once-locked fonts in Wiltshire, and there may be
many others. I find, too, that in all the places where such
fonts are found, there always seem to be barrows or tumuli,
or other relics of the Bronze Age, such as sarsen stones.
This possibly ties up with the belief that the craft of the
witch may have been handed down from those far-off
times, if the descendants of the Druids remained in the old
places. Traditionally the traits of the Druid were control
of the body (hypnosis, telepathy, auto-suggestion, de-
tached consciousness), control over animals, and a knack
with herbs. All these were traits of the witch. It was said
that with bare feet, loose hair, and robes tucked up round
their waists, the Druids gathered herbs in the light of the
new moon, from the north side of the hedge, and they
gathered and distilled using the left hand. Trees, groves,
springs, crossroads, and river boundaries were all their
holy places and also where sarsen stones lay. This, too,
applied to a witch.

I have heard that a coven called 'Moonrakers' a few
years ago still gathered at Gorse Hill near Swindon;[1] and
at the Devil's Den, not far from Avebury, very odd inci-

[1] Mrs. W. Rutter (from her sister-in-law).

dents were reported as recently as 1971. Someone visiting the huge dolmen at Clatford Bottom found feathers of wild birds scattered all around the cromlech, and a piece of cardboard, protected by polythene, was tied by string to a stone. On it someone had written an odd mixture of figures and letters – quite unintelligible to ordinary folk. And yet another visitor at another time found a dead hare – one of the sacred animals of both Druid and the witch – lying under the huge stones.

There are many tales of witches and witchcraft still told. It was general belief that horses were specially in danger from witches, who would take possession of the animals and ride them to their covens. In some fields it was not considered safe to have horses overnight (there was one, for instance, at Allington, near Devizes) or they would be in the morning found tired and muddy, with tangled mane and tail. Old Eli, the carter at Pennings Farm, Pewsey, told me that a witch rode a horse clutching mane and tail, and it was to prevent such liberties that horses were docked. Some horses had their tails and manes plaited, often with straw, in thirteen braids, and sometimes a tuft of red wool might be added.[2]

Less than a hundred years ago a part of the Wiltshire Downs where racehorses had their gallops was constantly troubled by a local witch. It was said (again, this is Old Eli) no lock or bar could prevent the opening of barn or stable doors – whether by muttered charm, or a corpse candle, or even a 'hand' – and the terrified horse was off to some distant orgy. Finally some of the braver local spirits caught the witch and lashed her with a horsewhip until

[2] Jim Hughes, gipsy, of Raffin, Pewsey.

they drew blood; thereafter her power was gone. It was common knowledge that should you draw blood from a witch 'above the breath' her power was lost.

Another well-known witch lived in a lonely place on Sedgemoor, where the counties of Somerset and Wiltshire meet. She was greatly feared by the local people, for she had bewitched the animals, stopped the butter-making, and generally disorganised all those against whom she bore a grudge. One of the signs of her displeasure was to cause a plague of fleas. These descended on several people in the district and it was more than the cleanly country house-wives could endure. They stormed off to the witch's lonely cottage, determined to rid themselves of her; but she saw them coming and fled up the huge old-fashioned chimney. Though this was the traditional way of exit, witches gener-ally made their way naked, only oiled with the witch oint-ment made from foxglove (to accelerate the pulse), aconite (to numb the feet and hands), and belladonna, cowbane, or hemlock (to confuse the senses), mixed with fat and maybe soot – a toxic ointment which reputedly gave the sensation of flying. This witch, however, forgot to remove her shift in her haste, and it caught fire; she pulled it off and threw it down the chimney, where it descended upon the advanc-ing crowd of women. The witch was never seen again, and her cottage became an inn, which is still called The Burnt Smock.[3] Some say the witch haunts the place still.

No doubt it was because of the chimney being used as a witch's way of exit that on some old houses a step-like protrusion can be seen near the top of the chimney – this

[3] Told to me at Urchfont Manor College of Adult Education by a lecturer from the University of Hull.

was known as a witch-seat, and it was hoped if this was provided the witch would not descend the chimney. But in case she did, large white circles made from whiting mixed with urine were drawn upon the hearths and these were thought to prevent any witch passing across.[4] In some places they still are used. Some women also drew branched half-circles around their floor – they were taking no chances![5]

Of all animals, perhaps the hare was most associated with witchcraft; and it was into the hare that the witch was most often said to transform. Dr. Margaret Murray gives the method of making this ritual-change by the recital of an incantation :

> 'I shall goe intill ane haire,
> With sorrow, and sych, and meikle caire,
> And I shall goe in the Divellis ham,
> Ay whill I com hom againe.'

To revert again to human form the words were :

> 'Hare, hare, God send thee care,
> I am in an hare's likeness just now,
> But I shall be in a woman's likeness even now.'

The only way to shoot this hare-witch was to make a bullet from a silver coin : the one most favoured was the silver florin piece which had a cross made by the royal arms upon it. The old silver groat was similarly marked. Using this the hare could be killed.

Mr. V. Dupree, of Melksham, told me he had seen the figure of a witch drawn on to a barn door; then silver

[4] Mr. D. W. L. Holloway, Church Lench.
[5] Mrs. Morrison, Bratton.

bullets were shot into it which were said to wound or kill the actual woman – or man – witch.

I was told also of six farmers who were shooting hares on the Earl of Radnor's Longford estate. A hare emerged from the lane (called Bally Hag Lane because of an old witch who lived in a nearby cottage and gathered herbs in the lane) and ran along the line of guns. The farmers were all good shots and each of them shot two barrels, but failed to stop her. One of them had a rather wild retriever bitch who chased the hare as far as the garden hedge of the cottage, then raced back, tail between legs. It was said that the old woman was not seen for some time, but when she was, she was very lame, and had bandages on her hands and neck. This farm was at Wick, near Downton, about six miles from Salisbury.[6]

There is a road leading from Manningford Beeches to Wilcot which is called Hare Street, and along this path it is said you may sometimes meet an old lady who died many years ago, but who was credited with having 'sold her soul to the Devil'.

Many village people still refuse to eat hares: one old lady many years ago said it was 'like eating your grandmother'. Also, if a hare was seen in a village street a fire was often said to have been caused. The village of Aldbourne has suffered badly from fires: in 1760, 'laid in ashes', 'in 1777 another', and a third in 1870. According to an old tale a hare was seen outside the first house to be destroyed.[7]

Pins (and it seems they must be new ones) always seem

[6] Mr. F. G. Lye, Cocklebury Farm, Wilcot.
[7] Ida Gandy, Upper Sixpenny, Aldbourne.

to be involved in village witchcraft. Here is a very strange tale, which my aunt[8] told me when I was a girl, and which had been told to her many years before by a man who came from the part of Wiltshire around the Bratton White Horse. Once, in his young days, this man was talking to a woman of his village, generally considered to be a wise woman, or white witch, and the conversation turned upon the possibility of communication with anyone at a distance – about which the man was very sceptical. He said the old lady picked an apple from a basket on her kitchen table and took from her dresser drawer a paper of new pins; then, having stuck a number (he did not say how many) into the apple up to the head of the pin, she turned to the man and asked if he knew her sister, who lived about four miles away. He said that he did and the wise woman replied she was sending a message to her to come to see her at once. Thereupon she lifted the hob from her kitchen fire and dropped in the apple, murmuring some words; then she turned again to the young man, saying if he looked in in an hour or two, he would meet her sister. Hardly knowing what to think, he returned later to the house and found the old lady sitting by her fire knitting. 'No visitor, I see,' he said, and just then came a knock on the door and there stood the younger sister. 'Are you all right?' she asked the old lady, 'I had such a queer feeling that you wanted me that I *had* to come over!'

Another story was told by Mr. Grant of Bishops Cannings. He said in his youth there was an old lady who told fortunes – 'and such'. One day four young men from Urchfont decided to ask her to tell their fortunes

[8] Mrs. John Draper, Oak Farm, Wilcot.

and on the way to her house one of the lads remarked, 'I wonder if the old . . . will be at home?' When they reached her house and knocked at the door, her voice came from within, saying, 'Come in, the old . . . *is* at home!'

I have encountered something of the kind myself, being hailed by one of these wise women as I entered a place, where she had *saved me a seat* next to herself; I had not known I was attending this gathering until a short while before.

A very different sort of tale was told to me a few years ago, but I was not told in which Wiltshire village this happened. An old lady named Jane Hethercot lived there and was said to be a witch by the village folk. Boys were sometimes given to calling rude things when she walked along the village street, and one day a particularly bad boy called Tommy Fry threw a stone as well, which grazed the old lady's cheek. She stopped in her walk, pointed a finger, and said, 'You throwed thic stone! You don't spake again till I say.' Nor did he – not for days! His mother at last called on the rector and asked his help, and he arranged a meeting in his study – Mrs. Fry, Tommy, himself and old Jane. Mrs. Fry said quite a lot, accusing the old lady of causing Tommy's dumbness. Old Jane looked at her with contempt and turned to the boy. 'Spake, boy,' she said, 'you can spake as well as I can, cain't 'ee?' And Tommy answered, 'Yes.' Was the dumbness caused by Tommy's wilfulness or old Jane's bewitchment?

I often wondered how these village witches were known, but once I was told a witch cannot cry – or at most she can only shed three tears – and all from her left eye.[9] But

[9] Mrs. Lovelock, Wootton Rivers.

a sure way to discover if someone you suspect is a witch is to place a walnut under her chair and if your surmise is correct, she will be unable to rise. The walnut had other properties, too: it could apparently fasten loose teeth, heal wounds, and cure bites of serpents and mad dogs.

Various amulets were thought to be protective against witches: amongst country folk two homely ones – salt and pins – were often used. A charm which combined them both was sometimes kept on the pantry shelf to guard the food – three needles, three pins, and three nails, in a jar of salt. And the horseshoe, so often nailed – horns up, of course – over the door, was sometimes first dropped into brine. A jar of salt was also often kept by the kitchen fire-place, so that a pinch might be thrown on to the flames when anyone suspected of the Evil Eye entered. (Is that why many old beams above the inglenook have a cavity called the salt-box?) A person who thought he was be-witched was advised to put the trimmings of his toenails, together with a wisp of hair from the person who had cast a spell, into the fire, whilst at the same time the poker was put in, and lifted out again when it was red hot. This was called 'branding the witch', thus breaking the spell.[10] It was said you could see the mark on the witch's body after this performance.

In 1973 there was much interest in Devizes regarding a somewhat macabre object connected with witchcraft. There was a suggestion – which came to nothing – by the Mayor of Devizes, Councillor Mrs. P. Rugg, that a mum-

[10] Mr. Grant, Bishops Cannings, says a piece of steel, white hot, was put into a churn, when butter refused to 'come', and this also branded the witch who caused the trouble (September 1974).

mified hand, said to be that of the last man hanged at Devizes, might be included in an exhibition arranged to mark the borough's demise. Hands were cut from a hanged man, generally footpad or highwayman, whose body had been dipped in pitch and hanged from a gibbet. It was said that such a hand enabled the possessor to enter houses to steal without fear of capture, as the hand caused deep sleep to come to all within. There is a tale of an old man with such a reputation who not many years ago lived in a Wiltshire village. He was said to have been suspected of being a thief, but never was convicted, and died in his bed in his thatched cottage, which he owned. A grandson to whom the cottage had passed later sold it to an 'incomer', who had the thatch removed in order to substitute tiles. In the thatch, just above the window of the old man's bedroom, was found a hand – I was told it was still in existence, but out of consideration for his family, who still lived in the neighbourhood, nothing was said about it; for this reason, they would not give either the name of the village or of the old man.

My grandmother used to tell such a tale about a hand being used by the robber of an inn near her home – he fixed a lighted candle in the hand but it was put out by a young girl called Bella, who threw a cupful of milk over it, and so broke the spell. The landlord and his wife awoke and caught the thief.

Another potent possession of many witches was a pendulum of witch-hazel wood which was strung on a thread of wool, linen, silk or hair (it had to be natural substance) from a rod of hazel wood. With this the witch could divine water, metal (lost articles) and many other things. Nowadays it can track a journey on a map, the map being used wrong side up, with pins marking the spot where the pendulum ceases to swing. It will also answer some questions by swinging the way the sun turns for assent, 'widdershins' (or against the sun) for negative, and to and fro movement if undecided. It can be strangely accurate in its findings. This pendulum will only 'work' for some; in many people's hands it just hangs limply from its string. I have found it works best for those of Celtic blood – Welsh, Irish or Scots, and maybe those of the West country. Is it Druid blood again?

It is said Druids sited many stones on hidden springs and, being water diviners, could tell if a boundary stone had been moved. Water diviners say trees often lean over towards a hidden spring, and that cattle often choose to have their calf (and other animals their young) in a spot where there is one; and it is a fact a cow will break through a hedge to reach the spot she has chosen to have her calf.

II

WISE WOMAN'S HERBAL

'The powre of herbs, both which can hurt and ease,
And which be wont t'enrage the restless sheepe,
And which be wont to work enternal sleepe.'

SPENSER

A-Z

The Rev. W. Zaprell Allan, writing in 1887 in the *Weekly Parish Paper* of Broad Chalke,[1] supposed no wise woman took the place there of 'old Dame Zargett, a most useful

---

[1] In the same publication were written recipes for cures of skin disease from garden daisies, and for coughs and colds made from the field daisy.

woman in the old days, with her knowledge of herbs and simples'. These country cures, the chief secret of the village wise woman, still intrigue the imagination.

In the old days the Nine Mystic Herbs were held in highest esteem. These were hellebore, rosemary, lavender, sage, comfrey, rue, wormwood, marjoram and vervain. Some people added verbena, mint and chamomile. It is said forty-two plants (flowers, leaves or berries) are still used in homoeopathic medicine today. My collection, I find, runs to nearly sixty, and I list them here in alphabetical order.

Angelica, the strongest protection against witchcraft, was also recommended for the relief of flatulence – 'good to repel wind and to strengthen the stomach' – and an infusion was used for all digestive troubles, such as colic and heartburn. Angelica, barm and peppermint, mixed in equal proportions and infused, was taken hot at night to relieve sore throats and promote sleep.

Barm, a herb known for over four centuries, is sometimes called 'the bee's plant' as the bees love its very insignificant little white flower. Beekeepers also used the plant to rub on the inside of their skeps.

Barm tea was said to be invaluable in cases of fever, and we are told of John Hussy of Sydenham, Kent, who lived to be 116 years old, that he took nothing for his breakfast for fifty years but barm tea, sweetened with honey. Barm wine is excellent to serve with cheese and biscuits. Infusions are taken to relieve headache, toothache and earache. A few drops on sugar relieves nausea and vomiting.

Betony is a soft, hairy, pretty woodland plant which grows some two feet high and its purple-red flowers bloom

from June to September. It is said the whole plant above
the ground is beneficial. The old herbalist-physicians said,
'Sell your coat, and buy betony', implying this was the one
herb you could not be without. It is still used in medicine,
and in the last war was said to surpass modern drugs in
healing wounds, particularly among airmen suffering from
burns. It is named after Beronice, the woman healed
by Christ of an issue of blood.

Black Bryony, sometimes called big root, had a number
of cures. Wiltshire country folk called it 'blackeye root'. It
was a popular relief for chilblains, the berries (and roots
also) being steeped in gin for application. These were used
as a stimulating plaster for gout, rheumatism and paraly-
sis. It was sometimes known as chilblain berry.

Black bryony was also one of the plants used by horsemen to condition their animals and make horses' coats
shine. The 'big root' was scraped and moistened and
added to the horse's bait, but it was dangerous to use too
much, as this could have disastrous results. An old couplet
ran :

> 'Bryony served too dry
> Blinded horses when they blew.'

Bramble, or *Blackberry*, was efficacious in healing
scalds. Nine bramble leaves were dipped in clear spring-
water, or water taken from a running stream, and singly
applied to the wound, the following chant being repeated
three times to each leaf :

> 'Three ladies came from the east,
> One brought fire, and two brought frost,
> Out with fire, and in with frost,

In the name of the Father, and of the Son,
    and of the Holy Ghost,
            Amen – Amen – Amen.'[2]

Bramble also heals boils and blackheads.

Chamomile, one of the oldest herbs and said to be used as long ago as 1262, eased pains if applied outwardly. Gardeners looked upon chamomile as a 'plant physician', restoring to health any sickly plant near which it grew. The double form was best for medicinal purposes. For fractious children, chamomile flowers, picked when the sun was shining, dried in the sun and kept in a close stoppered jar, were used. A draught containing ten heads of chamomile, over which a pint of barley water was poured and sweetened by a large tablespoonful of honey, was given to the child – a glass, hot, every night, and a glass, cold, each day.[3] For earache a bag of flannel was made and filled with chamomile heads. This was warmed by the fire, and the child held the bag over the aching ear. It was good also for toothache or any pain in the neck, and the flowers were made into a poultice for relief of pain. Chamomile tea was used for nausea and biliousness.

Another use for the flowers was to produce a yellow dye, and chamomile flowers were often used as a hair tonic – for fair hair only – and as a shampoo.

Coltsfoot is perhaps the world's oldest cough cure, infusions and decoctions of the herb being used. Indeed the Latin name of the plant (*tussilago farfara*) actually means 'cough dispeller'. Powdered coltsfoot was taken as snuff,

---

[2] From an old Wiltshire wise woman.
[3] From Mrs. Aldridge, Wootton Rivers.

and sometimes smoked as a herbal tobacco to relieve sinus congestion.[4]

The Wiltshire name is 'son before the father', as its small yellow flowers, much like small dandelions, bloom in March before the hoof-shaped large leaves appear. (These leaves explain another name for the plant – 'horse-hoof'.) Coltsfoot flowers are used for making wine, and very good this can be.

Cowslips, or St. Peter's wort or palsy wort, are a mild sedative – a few flower heads eaten raw, or in infusions, are anti-hysterical, and promote sleep. The spotted cowslip – Shakespeare says 'in those freckles live their savours' – is said to be a cure for spots. An ointment of cowslip flowers 'taketh away spots and wrinkles of the skin, sunburning and freckles and adds beauty exceedingly'; the flower heads were simmered in hog's lard, strained, and the liquid simmered again with fresh flowers twice more. Infusion of cowslips was said to give ease to pains in the back – 'it opens the passage of the urine'.

Cowslips also make a liqueur-like wine.

Daisy (Field) was a Wiltshire remedy for coughs and colds.[5] For immediate use, make a strong tea of them. For future use, put the flowers into a stew-jar, pour boiling water on them, cover tightly, and let them stand ten or twelve hours. Then strain.

Both the above are for internal use and can be made either from fresh or dried blooms. Good for infections of the lungs.

[4] H. J. Wiltshire, Rustic Farm, All Cannings, who smoked it in an acorn pipe, about 1895.

[5] See note II, 1.

Daisy (Garden). A decoction made from daisies is considered good for skin diseases, and for varicose veins. It is also for internal use.[6]

The *Dandelion*'s golden small sun-like flowers make the most favoured Wiltshire wine; these must be picked on a sunny day before 24th May. Dandelion roots were used as a substitute for coffee. Six or eight pounds of root, cleaned of earth, and the tops cut off, were hung up to dry. Then they were grated like ginger. A teaspoonful and a half was allowed to stand five minutes in a pot holding a pint and a half. Dried dandelion roots were ground and used for stomach and liver complaints; and dandelion tea was a remedy for colds and some rheumatic pains. The leaves were eaten as a salad.

Dill takes its name from an old Norse word *dilla*, to lull. Its seeds are mildly soporific, too mild to act upon an adult frame, but good as dill-water for babes. Oddly, it once had a sinister reputation as one of the most potent of the magic herbs – and black magic at that!

Elder is the witch's particular tree. Indeed, she was said to live in the tree at times, and this superstition may account for the disinclination of many old countrymen to cut it down – it was even said it could bleed if this was done. Small wonder apologies were made when cutting was attempted: 'Old gal, old gal, gi' Oi yer wood, an' when Oi be a tree, Oi'll gi' yer o' mine.'

Almost every part of the elder is used in herbal medicine. Decoctions of the roots were used to make a general kidney tonic, and the pith of the elder was boiled in lard to make an ointment for sprains. A lotion from elder

[6] See note II, 1.

flowers cured sore eyes, and beautified the complexion, taking away sunburn. Elder berries were used to treat colds – my grandmother infused them and made a syrup called 'elder rob' for sore throats. Flowers, leaves and berries were all used to treat catarrh, and were also good for rheumatism. Added to which, both elder flowers and berries make a white and a red wine respectively, the latter best mulled for a winter hot drink with cloves, ginger and nutmeg.

The fungus known as 'Jew's ear' which grows on elder bushes, was thought to help sore throats, quinsy, and 'strangulation'. (Is there here a connection with Judas Iscariot, who is said to have hanged himself on an elder tree?). An elder twig was used in Wiltshire as a cure for warts. And the log which tradition says was left in her bed, adorned with her nightcap, by a witch out on her unlawful occasions, was said to be either of elder or hawthorn.

Elecampane (called horseheal) was reputed to cure skin diseases in horses and mules and also scab in sheep – hence scabwort. The herb was a first-class cough medicine : roots were infused in white wine, and sugar or honey added; dried powdered roots were mixed with sugar and taken in teaspoonful doses, or you could make a candy by cooking the roots, then coating them with hot sugar syrup and leaving them to set.

Fennel is a very ancient herb, used by the Romans and by Anglo-Saxons. Leaves, seeds and roots were used in drinks or broth to make people 'more lean that are too fat'. It was added, 'Wild fennel is stronger than the tame – and hotter !' Seed heads of both fennel and dill were carried to church to nibble during the long service, and were known as 'meeting seeds'. The juice of the fennel in wine was said to be 'good against the swellyings of the dropsye', and a plaster of fennel root was applied for the bites of mad dogs. Country lore said, 'Sow fennel, sow sorrow' – and if you gave it away, disaster would follow.

Fern (adder's tongue) is said to cure sore eyes.

Fleabane. In the days when the floors of houses were strewn with rushes, fleabane was regularly burned in the rooms to drive out fleas and other insect invaders. The Arabs used to call the fleabane by the name of 'Job's tears', believing that Job used the plant to ease his painful ills during the time of his afflictions. Grazing animals appear to avoid it.

Foxglove is a somewhat deadly plant, but used by some old healers and in constant use in today's pharmacopoeia. The story is told of an Oxford don, given up by his doctor in the last stage of dropsy, who went to see his old home in Shropshire for the last time. Here he met and was treated by the village wise woman, and was cured. When he returned to Oxford in good health his doctor went to see the woman and eventually managed to buy her remedy. This is said to have occurred in 1775, and in 1785 Dr. Withering wrote 'Account of the Foxglove' – the Shropshire witch's cure.

In country districts a strong infusion of the leaves was applied warm to the abdomen. And to counteract the deleterious effects of an overdose we are told to use laudanum in brandy, water or a strong infusion of green tea. Nightshade was used for scrofulous tumours (king's evil), spasmodic asthma and epilepsy. For deafness, the juices of the bruised flowers, leaves and stalks of fresh foxgloves were mixed with double quantity of brandy and kept for use. If made in June the preparation would keep for a year. One drop was put in the ear at night, a piece of lint was moistened with it and put into the ear, and taken out next morning.

Foxglove was one ingredient of the witch's 'toxic flying ointment', and it was said to accelerate the pulse.

Gorse is the golden flower of which it is said that 'kissing be out of season when gorse be out of bloom'. It is the Wiltshire cure for dropsy, the flowers infused and taken as a tonic. This was told by an old shepherd of the Plain.

The *Hawthorn* is the second special tree of the witch, yet much used in cures. The distilled water of hawthorn flowers was said to draw both thorns and blisters from the skin. Wine was made from the creamy white blossoms in May and also from the red fruits in autumn (the haws), both of which – and also a tea – were good heart tonics, and beneficial also for asthma and for dropsy. An infusion of the flowers was good for sore throats.

In Wiltshire it was thought unlucky to bring mayblossom into a house as it presaged a death, but this was only when used as a decoration, not as a cure.[7] This legend is said to go back to druidical, possibly predruidical, days, when a young man and maiden were chosen as a perfect couple, and for the whole succeeding year were feted as king and queen, and then put to death at the year's end. The doomed couple were crowned at their inauguration with mayblossom – hence its association with death.

Wiltshire children used to eat hawthorn leaves, which they called 'bread and cheese'.

[7] Miss Dorothy Amer, Pewsey.

Hazel. The nuts are good for curing coughs and are also supposed to help prevent hardening of the arteries.

Henbane is one of the most virulent poisons ever used by a witch, yet in constant use in today's pharmacopoeia. Hyoscine, derived from henbane and known as 'twilight sleep', has brought to women in childbirth, or victims of shattering nervous collapse, the relief of temporary oblivion.

Herb Bennet, sometimes called avens or colewort, was said to be of 'sweet flavour and warming quality', a decoction of powdered root being taken in wine for stomach disorders and poisons, bites and stitches in the sides. It was also used as a spring pick-me-up taken in boiling water. It was said these roots should be dug on 25th March, from dry ground.

The herb bennet was the gipsy's fragrant 'kind herb', and they say it is needed and sought by all animals.[8] It was used for veterinary treatment for jaundice (the 'yellow' in hounds), dysentery and digestive ailments. In the old days it was also used to flavour ale.

Houseleek. If warts are rubbed with crushed houseleek leaves they disappear.[9] Lesser celandine, houseleek and plantain, made into an ointment in hog's lard, is excellent for curing piles.

Hyssop, said to have been used before 1440, is a well-known bee-plant, the blue flowers being a great attraction. Its uses are many : country folk bruised the leaves with sugar and applied them to a green wound with much success; the leaves applied with warm water take away blue

[8] Jim Hughes, Pewsey (gipsy).
[9] Mrs. G. Parrott, Upper Minety, September 1971.

or black spots caused by strokes or falls; boiled with rue and honey it relieves coughs and shortness of breath; and it assists to expectorate phlegm.

Hyssop, with barm and a small quantity of mint, was used to brew a wholesome tea, and a handful of dried hyssop in a linen cloth immersed in boiling water was considered a sovereign application to a black or a bloodshot eye. It was also thought to avert the Evil Eye.

Ivy cured a multitude of evils. The leaves were soaked in vinegar and bound on to corns or bunions. Lotions were made for sore eyes by soaking ivy leaves in water. This lotion was also used for skin rashes. For jaundice, roots of ground ivy were boiled in water for the patient to drink. Taken in wine, the white ivy berries were said to help to break up the stone, provoke urine, and women's courses. To avert the effects of heavy drinking, a decoction of ivy leaves and berries was used; and for whooping cough food or drink was given in an ivy-wood bowl. To cure a heavy cold, juice pressed from the leaves was snuffed up the nose, and the wearing of an ivy wreath was recommended to prevent loss of hair.

Juniper berries are said to 'give appetite to the most jaded'. Infusions of twigs and berries are good for stones and gravel, and also for flatulence. The berries are also used to flavour gin.

Lavender. Infusions of the flowers make a soothing nerve tonic and are said to get rid of nervous headaches. Some say a sprig of lavender worn under your hat will help.[10] To make a kind of lavender water to ease head-

---

[10] Mrs. M. E Denton.

aches, two tablespoonfuls of dried lavender flowers, a table-spoonful of sweet cicely leaves, a big pinch of nutmeg and a teaspoonful of cinnamon are powdered together and mixed with a quart of surgical spirit. This is allowed to steep for a week or more, then it is strained and bottled, and sealed very tightly so that it is ready for use when needed. Used on cloths wrung out in cold water to ease headaches or fevers, it is very refreshing and cooling.

Lily of the Valley. Infusions of the leaves or decoctions of the roots were taken in small doses night and morning as a calming nerve tonic, and it was also reckoned to strengthen the memory. It was thought to be a good tonic remedy after strokes, and helped to restore lost speech and reduce high blood pressure.

Madonna Lily is said to be the oldest domesticated plant – it is represented on Cretan vases and other objects of the middle Minoan period, between 1750 and 1600 B.C. It was known to the Assyrians and probably carried westward by the Phoenicians. It was considered a cure for corns, a treatment for dropsy, and was used for erysipelas and for quinsy. It cured burnings and scaldings without a scar and the petals, steeped in brandy, were used to cure bruises. (This last was my husband's grandmother's[11] cure for his brother and himself when small boys.)

The *Marigold* was the 'golds' of ancient literature, and like nearly all yellow flowers was protective as it reflected the sun. In more recent times, the juice of marigold leaves mixed with vinegar was said to 'give ease to hot swellings', and an infusion of the flowers taken regularly was excellent for catarrh. The juice of marigolds frequently applied

[11] Mrs. Elizabeth Thomas, Studley, near Calne.

was effectual in removing warts, and mixed with a small portion of spirits of wine (or even without) was a rare application for healing lacerations, bruises and cuts, both pain and bleeding being arrested and seldom leaving a scar. Infusions of the flowers were taken internally as a safe remedy for varicose veins and it is generally good for the circulation. The infusion was also used as a lotion to bathe varicose veins and ulcers to promote healing.

An old-time maid of Mrs. Crees, of Manor Farm, All Cannings, said that in the 1860s her mistress used to boil marigold flowers in milk, which she sweetened with honey, and gave to her children to drink when they were suffering from measles.[12]

Marigolds were said to have been woven in amongst the corn-ears which formed the 'corn-dolly' made at harvest time.[13]

Marjoram was one of the old 'cure-alls'. It was put into home-brewed beer to give it scent and savour, and a marjoram tea was a remedy against infections of the lungs and chest. A few drops of strong infusion, warmed, were put into the ear several times a day to melt wax, and were reputed to reduce pain. Oil of marjoram was sometimes substituted for oil of cloves to drop into an aching tooth. It was also said to correct mild indigestion.

My grandmother used an infusion of marjoram as a fragrant mouthwash, and it was also used in making soaps and sweet waters. Taken as an infusion two or three days before and up to the usual date, marjoram will regularise menstruation.

[12] Mrs. Cornelius Hiscock, 1947.
[13] Miss Ruth Tongue.

There was an old country saying that marjoram would only grow on a grave if the departed was happy.

Decoctions of the root of the *Marsh Mallow* formed part of many herbal cough medicines, as it soothes and heals inflammation, and it was also used for kidney treatment, and as a lotion for swollen or uncomfortable breasts. An old recipe ran, 'Take an ounce of marsh mallow roots, and two or three figs, and boil in a quart of water, till near half of it be consumed, then strain and add an ounce of honey and half an ounce of water of ammonia. It will then be an exceeding good gargle, beneficial in fevers. For a sore throat, two parts wine to six ounces of water, and two tablespoonfuls of this vinegar.'

Milder is said to have been used as a vegetable from pre-historic days. Indeed, the name Mildenhall (a Roman station in Suffolk and Wiltshire) is supposed to derive its name from this plant. Its leaves resemble those of spinach, it is mildly purgative and a potent source of iron. It was sometimes called 'fat hen', being used to feed and fatten hens. Another of its names, 'Good King Henry', refers to the German sprite Heinz or Heinrich – our Robin Good-fellow – and apparently has nothing to do with any King Henry – the Eighth or otherwise. It was also called 'English mercury' or 'all good'.

Mint is perhaps the best known of all herbs. Pliny wrote, 'The smell of mint doth stir up the mind and the taste to greedy desire of meat. Mint is marvellous wholesome for the stomach. It is good against watering eyes, if poured into the ears with honeyed water.' The old village wise woman also held that mint infusions taken regularly would treat infertility and regularise menstruation, while goldenrod and mint infused together were used to relieve morning sickness. Peppermint was brewed as a tea by my grand-mother and used for any pain in the stomach, or period pains. Mint was also a cure for hiccups.

Mistletoe, the 'golden bough' which opened the gate-way to Hades, was accorded special reverence by the Druids, especially when found growing on an oak – which happens rarely. It was gathered by the Druid with his feet bare, and as it must neither be touched by hand nor cut by iron, it was cut by a bronze or golden knife, and caught in a white cloth as it fell. The mistletoe is usually found on either apple, oak or hawthorn trees, very rarely on a pear tree.

An old recipe for 'Violent Epilepsy' says, 'Take as much powdered mistletoe as would lie on a sixpence early in the morning in black cherry water, or beer, for some days near the full moon.' Another herbalist advised, 'Three or four mistletoe berries, eaten when fasting, night and morning, are anti-hysterical, but mistletoe is strong medicine and not for children,' and 'Pound up a handful of mistletoe berries and rub them on stiff joints and swellings, to re-lieve pain. For external use only.' Strong infusions are a mild heart tonic, and help to relieve blood pressure and stitch.

Mugwort – or felon herb (felons were abscesses or gatherings) – had many virtues ascribed to it. It was one of the plants hung above the house door on Midsummer Day to scare witches and the Devil; it also warded off lightning. The power of mugwort was so strong that if it was laid under the door, neither man nor woman could annoy in that house; and another strange theory ran that the herb's leaves were always turned to the north. As this was always considered to be the Devil's quarter, one wonders why.

An old lady at Wootton Rivers, near Marlborough, had a much more practical use for the herb; she brewed from it a spring tonic (and another from young nettles).

> 'If they took muggins in March,
> And nettles in May,
> So many fair lassies
> Wouldn't lie in cold clay.'

Present-day herbalists say mugwort provokes and enhances menstrual flow.

Mullein, the tall herb with yellow flowers and large flannel-like leaves, was considered to be a first-class cough cure, taken in infusions. Country folk had another way of using the plant. For a sore neck, swollen glands, mumps, etc., they made a strong brew of leaves and flowers, and brought it almost to the boil. Then vinegar was added, and this liquid was used as a fomentation, dipping a clean cloth in it, and wrapping it round the neck. Infusions were also taken, as they were considered soothing to the kidneys.

Nettles seem, for all their unpopularity, to be of great use in herb medicine. The whole plant from roots to seeds has its uses. It is a fine general tonic, eaten as a vegetable like spinach or taken in infusions; and it makes a liqueur-like wine. It is said to be particularly good for the gout, and for glandular ailments.

Nettles were applied as a cure for dandruff, an infusion being massaged in daily, or essential oil made from stinging nettles rubbed into the scalp. They were also used as a

face-pack — the leaves chopped, crushed and simmered
for about ten minutes, with just enough water to keep
them from burning. Then the herb was spread on thin
muslin, and slapped straight on to the face. After fifteen
minutes it was removed and the face washed with warm
water and lemon juice.

As a 'blood purifier', gather tops of young nettles, wash
well, and to each pound add one quart of water. Boil for
an hour, strain, to each pint of juice add one pound of
sugar. Boil up again for thirty minutes. When cold, bottle
up.

The *Onion* is a country cure for a cold, often as onion
soup made with hot milk, and many cottage women used
to keep a cut onion under the sink to attract any germ
which might be about. They also thought snakes had a
strong antipathy to the smell of onions, and a raw onion
carried in hand was protection against attack.

Mrs. John Lloyd, of Great Bedwyn, Wiltshire, told me
her husband, a great bee-keeper, always used onion-juice
on the sting of a bee – or a wasp. It was an old bee-keeper's
remedy.[14]

Parsley is one of the most magical plants known. Why it
is so connected with the Devil has always been a mystery
to me. Old gardeners would tell you that parsley must be
sown on Good Friday – a rising moon was essential. You
must sow four times the amount of seed you require, to
give the Devil his quota. Even then the seed has to go down
nine times to the Devil before it can germinate – which is
why it seems slow to appear. In some parts it was thought
only the mistress of the house should sow parsley, but

[14] I used this remedy in September 1974, and it was effective.

others hold that should any woman do so, she at once becomes pregnant. But all seem to agree that parsley must never, never be transplanted : dire disaster will overtake the household if it is. I well remember the horror of an old Wiltshire woman when I asked for a root of her flourishing parsley bed.

It is one of the plants used to procure abortions by witches, and eaten raw or made into strong infusions was an excellent bladder-tonic. It is sometimes called 'the Devil's oatmeal', and apparently 'only the wicked' can grow it. In any case, I make a wonderfully good wine from this herb, which many folk enjoy!

Pennyroyal, the smallest of the mints, was used in infusions for all chest and lung complaints. An old herbal states, 'A garland worn about the head is of great force against the swimming of the head and giddiness thereof.' It was used to regularise menstruation, but must never be used by a pregnant woman. In remote country districts it was often used to procure abortions, as well as by gipsies, who sometimes peddled a decoction of pennyroyal for this purpose with their pegs and other wares.

Periwinkle, the old herbalists' 'juy of grownde' (joy of the ground and used against 'Devil sickness, snaky wild beasts, poisons, and that thou mayest have grace') was also recommended for making fast loose teeth, and considered 'a great binder' – chewing the leaves stayed bleeding at mouth and nose. It was used in an ointment for bleeding piles, and as an infusion to stay women's courses. Worn about the calf of the leg, it cured cramp. An early recipe for a poultice reads : 'Take fresh periwinkle leaves, spread them on brown paper, cover them with combed flax and fumigate all with frankincense.' Yet this is the same plant that was once called the 'sorcerer's violet'. Maybe that is why medieval malefactors in England were garlanded with it when on their way to the gallows.

The somewhat rare red periwinkle is said to have been the origin of 'the pink of perfection' and if planted outside the garden gate is an open invitation to passers-by to come in and look at the garden.

Plantain – or waybroad – was another 'cure-all' : an eleventh-century book of recipes prescribes it for twenty-two diseases. Its common name of waybroad was acquired from a legend about a maiden who was always looking for her absent lover, until at last she was changed to a plant always found by the wayside. Since then, every seventh year it becomes a cuckoo. Later, the plant was given an additional name of 'Englishman's foot', as it was said to spring up wherever an Englishman trod.

Plantain was a wound herb, and the leaves were used for external application to ulcers. It was good for inflammation of the intestines, diarrhoea and piles, as it had a soothing effect. The seeds of the plantain may be eaten dry, sprinkled on salads, or washed down by water, or an infusion may be made of the leaves, but the seeds are the strongest. Juice from the plant was put into hollow teeth to allay pain. In South Carolina an Indian received an award for giving plaintain as a cure for rattlesnake bite.

Raspberry leaf tea was an old countrywoman's cure for relieving morning sickness and it was also said to help labour. The berries can also be so used. It was thought it should be taken regularly throughout pregnancy because its special influence on the muscles of the pelvic region and uterus might help attain easy childbirth. It was also reputed to increase fertility. It is one of the most important female medicines.

Rosemary was used for aiding the toilet. For a hair wash 'take two ounces of glycerine, one spoonful of borax, mix, then fill the bottle with rosemary water'.[15] I, more simply, pick from my rosemary bush a good handful of leaves, which I put into a large old china teapot and fill it up with boiling water – just as you make tea. After allowing it to become cold I use the liquid as the last rinse when I wash my hair. Not only does it darken the hair and make it shine, it also imparts a faint perfume.

An old herbal says, 'Boyle the leaves in white wine, and wash thy face therewith, and thy browes, and thou shalt have a fair face'; 'Put the leaves under thy bedde, and thou shalt be delivered of evil dreams'; 'Put the flowers in thy chest among thy clothes and books, and moths shall not destroy them'; 'Make a box of Rosemary wood and smell it oft, and it shall preserve thy youth'; 'Sleep on a pillow stuffed with Rosemary for eternal youth.'

There were many remedies from this herb, too. For a cough, drink water of the leaves boiled in white wine. This was also good for loss of appetite. For gout, the leaves were applied, bound in a linen cloth. Rosemary was said to be a good tonic for the reproductive system, and a supreme heart tonic – infusions were used to treat heart ailments, and also high blood pressure. It was a good digestive and would cure mild forms of indigestion.

Rue – the herb of grace – was said to be twice as valuable if stolen from someone else's garden. It was thought to have

15 Mrs. Hannah Stainer.

been the antidote which Mercury gave Ulysses to counteract the drink offered by Circe. It was then called moly. No wonder country folk believed that if the floor of the house was rubbed with rue, all witches would fly from it.

Wicked nuns supposedly used rue as a contraceptive, eating copiously of the leaves before orgies began. Village women certainly used rue to regularise menstruation, infusing a small teaspoonful of dried herb to half a pint of water, which was taken twice daily in tablespoonful doses. Rue was also used as a heart and artery tonic, when infusions were taken in very small doses, a small teaspoonful to half a pint of water – it is a herb that can upset some people. The herb was thought to remove the formation of deposits in tendons and joints, so was particularly useful in treating arthritis, lumbago and sciatica, and very small doses of the infusion were used to relieve cramp. It was also a remedy for croup in fowls.[16]

'*Sage* set in May will never decay', one old gardener told me, and added that it 'likes to grow' with marjoram. Another old belief was that if rue be planted with sage, it will prevent the sage being poisoned by toads. According to local folklore the sage will prosper while the master is well, while the Arabs have a saying, 'How can a man die who has Sage in his garden?' John Evelyn agrees, for he says, ' 'Tis a plant indeed with so many and wonderful properties as that the assiduous use of it is said to render men immortal.'

Infusions of sage, mixed with honey and vinegar, were used as a soothing medicine for sore throats. A pint of boiling water was poured upon twenty or thirty leaves,

[16] Mrs. J. Draper, Oak Farm, Wilcot.

and allowed to stand for half an hour. Enough vinegar was added to the strained liquid to make it moderately acid, with honey according to taste. The dose was a tea-spoonful when necessary and could be used as a gargle several times a day.[17] The infusion was a helpful cold remedy, corrected mild forms of indigestion and was even used to increase milk-flow in nursing mothers.

An old herbal says, 'Sage is of excellent use to help the memory, warming and quickening the senses. A conserve made of the flowers is used to the same purpose. It also causeth the hair to become black.' My grandmother made a hair tonic of sage combined with rosemary for dark hair, and she also held that teeth rubbed with sage leaves became very white. And sage leaves, yarrow and old ale were recommended for a 'gnawing at the heart'.

St. John's Wort, the pleasant golden flower in the garden, often called 'Rose of Sharon' in Wiltshire,[18] was so detested by witches that pious folk hung pieces of the herb over the doorways of their dwellings on St. John's Eve (23rd June) to keep the witches away. Another legend went that if on the eve of St. John the Baptist's Day you stepped on the plant, a fairy horse would arise out of the ground, who would carry you gloriously all night but would leave you, wherever you might be, directly the first rays of the rising sun stirred the world.

The plant was said to be a sure preservative against tempests, thunderstorms, and all evil spirits. It was also an antidote to snake-bite and a protection against hydrophobia. Freshly gathered leaves were bruised and used to

[17] Mrs. Anne Secker, 1828.
[18] The late Mrs. Freda Hawkins, All Cannings.

bind on wounds and hurts; or were made into an ointment to close cuts and wounds. Decoctions of the seeds were taken warm to cure sciatica, and infusions were considered a general liver and stomach remedy.

Sorrel is the source of the poison salts of lemon, and also oxalic acid, yet infusions of the leaves are good for kidney disorders and, mixed with a little honey, the same infusion taken in small doses will relieve throat and mouth ulcers. And as children we chewed the leaves if we were thirsty!

Southernwood – more often known as 'lad's love', or 'old man', or 'maiden's ruin' – was said to possess one hundred virtues. Boiled with bread and roasted quinces it cured inflammation of the eyes, it was said to draw forth splinters, and 'helps those whose hair has fallen out, and are bald'.

A lady of sixty once told me that when she was first married her mother-in-law had told her how her grandmother had mixed her many a drink of 'lad's love' when her periods were late. Southernwood is also said to help asthma, to keep away moths, and to dye wool yellow.

Tansy, being one of the 'everlasting' flowers, was in olden days laid upon a corpse, in the belief the plant would transmit its lasting element to the dead body, particularly when relatives had to travel long distances to attend the funeral.

An old herbal runs : 'Fried with eggs as is the custom in Spring helpeth to digest and carry downward the bad humours that trouble the stomach. Being boiled in oil it is good for the sinews shrunk by cramp or pained with cold.' It was quoted, 'Tansy for childbearing', and the herb was bruised and applied to the navel to prevent miscarriage. It was used also as a general tonic in all heart weaknesses and for coughs and chest complaints, taken in small doses of weak infusions; and externally as a lotion for varicose veins. Tansy tea was given to children in the spring and was used as a cosmetic wash to remove sunburn. A brilliant yellow dye could be obtained from the herb, but this was difficult to 'fix'.

Thorn Apple or datura is said to have been brought to Britain in prehistoric times from Mediterranean countries for magic and medical use. The white-flowered plant is still often used – smoked like tobacco – as a remedy for asthma. It grows in wild places and, when in fruit, displays the rather large seed-vessels covered with spines or thorns from which it derives its name. It is a poison, but can be used as a valuable soother of pain or irritation.

Thyme, which is credited with one hundred species, has been used since the time of the Assyrians. Our ancestors called it 'the merry herb', perhaps because of its lively flavour and stimulating scent. The essential oil is a disinfectant more than twelve times as powerful as carbolic acid.

Thyme tea and honey were given for whooping cough, and an infusion of the leaves was good for asthma. An ointment made from thyme was used for 'hot swellings', warts, and pains in the back. Infusions were good for coughs and catarrhal troubles and regularised menstruation. Leaves were considered a remedy against bee-stings, 'if bruised and laid thereon'.

Vervain was one of the herbs held most sacred by the Druids and is believed to be verbena. Vervain 'must be picked at Spring o'day in ye month of May' – uprooting was to be performed at the rising of the day-star, when neither sun nor moon was shining, and it must be lifted with the left hand. No metal must touch the plant so it was usually dug by the tine of a stag's antler. Libations of honey were offered to the earth when the vervain was dug.

In addition to giving protection from witchcraft, the plant was said to cure scrofula and the bites of rabid animals, foil poison, avert 'antipathies', and be used as a pledge of mutual good faith.

It was said to be a 'cure-all', and a splendid tonic for all the ills of man, especially nervous complaints. Infusions were used to treat jaundice, and for chest troubles, coughs and colds.

Old 'blood-staunchers' used vervain, saying this as it was dug:

'Hallowed be thou, Vervain, as thou growest on the ground,
For in the mount of Calvary there thou wast first found.
Thou healest our Saviour, Jesus Christ, and staunchest his
    bleeding wound,
In the name of Father, Son and Holy Ghost, I take thee from
    the ground.'

The beautiful sweet-scented *Violet* was in much demand as a 'simple' by the old herbalists. Violet leaves were infused and made into a 'tea' which was particularly good for headaches, and an infusion of flowers – one pound to two and a half pints of boiling water – was used for stomach inflammations, because of its cooling effect on the mucous membranes. Raw leaf poultices, or ointment of leaves and flowers pulped raw into cold cream, were used to treat swollen glands. A sock was then used as a poultice bandage round the throat. An infusion of violets was also considered a good gargle.

But it was as 'a safe and gentle purger of young children' that the flower came into most use. Here is an old recipe : 'Syrope of Vyolettes is made in this manner. Sethe vyolettes in water and let it lye all night in the same water. Then poure and streyne out the water, and in the same pot put sugar and make your syrope. Oyle of Vyolettes : Sethe vyolettes in oyle and streyne it. It will be oyle of vyolettes.'

The herb *Wormwood* is supposed to have sprung up along the path through which the serpent wound its way in the Garden of Eden, hence its bitter taste and its name. It is one of the 'bitter herbs' mentioned in the Bible, but the Saxons used wormwood to flavour their beer. The wild species is often called mugwort still for this reason.

A salve made from wormwood was used to aid 'one suffering from nocturnal goblin visitors' – and it was also said to keep away fleas ! As these insects were thought to be sent as a plague by a witch, this also ties up with the old belief that witches were said to abhor wormwood, so much so that the herb was sometimes called the 'girdle of St. John', and used to keep evil at bay.

Yarrow has been known and used as a 'wound herb' for many ages. It has been used in this country since 1440, but the old story told that yarrow was used by Achilles, instructed by Chiron the centaur.

Its uses were many and varied. It was used in ale instead of hops 'to increase the inebriating quality of the liquor', while yarrow tea, sweetened with honey or treacle and with a little cayenne pepper added, was thought to be a good remedy for colds. Infusions of the herb were used for rheumatism, measles, jaundice and kidney disorders, and the green leaves were chewed to quell toothache. To ease earache, warm infusion was dropped into the ears, or even a crushed wad of leaves put into the ear.

An ointment which cured green wounds and other sores was made from freshly gathered tops of shoots stewed in hog's lard, and a decoction made by boiling flowers and tops of shoots in water for a short time was used to arrest loss of hair.

FOLK CURES

Here is the wise woman's remedy for hay fever, which was known then as 'flying venom'. This was said to be particularly dangerous for 'fifteen nights ere Lammas (1st August) and after it for five and thirty nights' (this would be from 17th July to 5th September).

'*A Salve for Flying Venom*: Take a handful of hammerwort, and a handful of maythe (chamomile), and a handful of waybroad (plantain), and the roots of water dock, seeking those which will float, and one eggshell-full of clean honey. Then take clean butter, and let him who will help to work up the salve melt it thrice. Let one sing a Mass over the worts, before they are put together, and the salve be wrought up.'

Plague Vinegar : Four malefactors who robbed and murdered people infected during the course of the plague owned at the gallows that they had preserved themselves from the contagion by this remedy alone, and that they went to all the houses without fear. They were pardoned for the discovery. 'Take of rue, sage, mint, rosemary, wormwood and lavender, a handful of each. Infuse them together in a gallon of white wine vinegar. Put the whole into a stone pot, closely covered up and pasted over the cover. Set the pot thus covered up upon warm wood ashes for eight days, after which draw off and strain through french flannel the liquid. Put it into quart bottles, and into every bottle put a quarter of an ounce of camphire. With this preparation wash your mouth, and rub your loins and temples, every day, snuff a little up your nostrils when you go into the air and carry a bit of sponge dipped in it to smell occasionally.' (This remedy was taken from an old leather-bound handwritten book, the property of the Misses Stuart, Potterne, dated 1797.)

There is an old story (told by the late Mr. Herbert Giddings) that three men left London in 1644, hoping to escape the plague. They were John, Jacob and Humphrey Giddings. They reached Urchfont village, and found they had brought the illness with them, so they dug themselves three graves on Wickham Green, or Workforth Common, in the middle of a large open field about a mile from Urchfont Manor. These can still be seen. One of the brothers was said to have recovered and from him all the people named Giddings have descended.

Recipe for Rheumatism : Mix well together one ounce each of spirits of wine, camphor and hartshorn, with half an ounce of turpentine.

Eno's Fruit Salts : Sieve and mix very well together two ounces each of Epsom salts, cream of tartar, tartaric acid, and carbonate of soda, one ounce of magnesia and half a pound of castor sugar. I have made this and found it excellent. (My grandfather said his father always kept a bottle of these salts on his bedside table. Great-grandfather died in 1860.)

Grandfather's Cold Cure : Take four new-laid eggs, put narrow ends downward in a jar, and squeeze the juice of four lemons over them. Turn them every day until the eggshells have dissolved – about six to eight days – then beat all up and add a quarter of a pound of sugar candy and one pint of rum. Take a wineglassful fasting, or when the cough is troublesome. (My aunt told me it was troublesome surprisingly often.)

'Two walnutts and two figges and twenty rue leaves stamped together with a little salt, and eaten fasting, will defend a man from pestilence and poison that day.'

Cure for an Ague : Take as much snuff of a candle as would lie on a sixpence, and make into an electuary with honey.

Cure for Sprain :[19] Take a large spoonful of honey, one of salt, and the white of an egg. Beat the whole up incessantly for two hours (*sic*). Let it stand for an hour, then anoint the part strained with the oil which will have been produced. Keep the part well rolled with a bandage.

Cure for Stiffness of Joints : Beat quite thin the yoke of a new-laid egg and add, a spoonful at a time, three ounces of pure water, agitating it continually. This to be applied to the contracted part, either cold, or milk-warm, rubbing for a few minutes, three or four times a day.

A Remedy for Colic (excellent and quick-acting) :[20] A mixture of a pinch each of ground cloves, allspice, ginger and cinnamon in a little brandy, gently warmed.

[19] Mrs. Harriet Draper.
[20] Mrs. E. M. Denton.

Cough Mixture :[21] One large teaspoonful of linseed, one ounce of liquorice root, quarter of a pound of raisins, two quarts of water, quarter of a pound of brown sugar candy, one tablespoonful of white wine vinegar or lemon juice. Boil together linseed, liquorice and raisins with water until the quantity is reduced by half. Strain off, and add the rest of the ingredients while the liquid is still hot. Stir it all very well. Drink half a pint before going to bed or take a large dose whenever the cough is troublesome.

Chilblain Cures : Make a thin mixture of mustard and brandy – half an eggcupful of brandy to a teaspoonful of mustard. Dress the chilblains and leave to dry. Only to be applied to unbroken chilblains. Another cure was a mixture of cayenne pepper and vinegar.

Absolute Cure for Ringworm :[22] Put one penny in vinegar. Twenty-four hours later take the penny out, and anoint the ringworm with the vinegar until it has gone. This was sometimes also used as a cure for warts.

A Remedy for Wounds : Samile, milfoil and bugle, steeped in white wine.

A Farmhouse Salve :[23] Put a good handful each of elder-flowers, wormwood and groundsel into an earthenware pot with one pound of home-rendered unsalted lard. Bring to the boil in the oven, and simmer for half an hour. Strain into pots and tie down. This is good for cows' udders, as also was goose-grease.

A Good Liniment :[24] One cupful each of vinegar and turpentine, a piece of camphor and one egg are mixed

[21] Mrs. Harriet Draper.
[22] Mrs. Brett.
[23] Mrs. Harriet Draper.
[24] Mrs. M. E. Denton.

together in a bottle until white and creamy. This is good for chilblains and sprains.

For Lumbago : Boil small potatoes until soft in their skins. Strain and mash on to a large piece of flannel. Put this into your bed on an old blanket then lie on your back in the mash (*sic*).

SPELLS AND CHARMS

We still have a wart-curer in our village. He does not even have to see the person seeking his aid : all he must know is the number of warts. How he works his cure he refuses to divulge, nor how long it may take – that depends, he says, 'on wind and weather'.

Other wart cures are many. I was told recently of a cure of a gipsy horse-dealer, who required another man in the inn at Worton to buy the warts from the sufferer for two pennies. They all disappeared – nor did the buyer have the warts. A common Wiltshire way is to cut notches on an elder twig, one for each wart, and the twig is then buried, or 'put down the "privy" ', as one person said. Another way is to rub the warts with the inner skin of a broad bean pod (told by Mrs. Harry Gay), or a piece of house leek (from Mrs. Parrott, Hankerton). Both of these have proved effective. One person (Mrs. C. Mullett, All Cannings) told me she had *stolen* a piece of fat meat, with which she rubbed each wart, the meat being thrown over the left shoulder at a cross-roads. All this was done in secret and silence – and it worked.

Other charms are rather more spectacular. Cramp has almost as many cures as those prescribed for warts. One directs the sufferer from cramp to recite :

'The devil is tying a knot in my leg,
St. Peter! St. Peter! unloose it, I beg!'

This charm has apparently been known to work even when
the cramp was in another part of the body.

Another cure directed that you carry a bone from a
sheep – the 'cramp-bone' – in your pocket, or keep it under
the pillow. Some people advocated keeping a magnet in
the bed, or even tied to the ankle; others said you should
leave your shoes under your bed in the form of a cross.

The following charm was repeated by the wise woman
for the cure of sprains:

'Our Saviour rade – this forefoot slade,
Our Saviour lighted down,
Sinew to sinew – joint to joint – blood to blood – bone to bone,
Mend thou in God's name!'

A linen thread was tied about the injured part after
the solemn repetition of the charm, and called the 'wristing
thread' – maybe because the wrist, or ankle, was the part
to which it was most commonly applied.

My grandfather used to relate the tale of the only time
he saw an old country blood-stauncher's charm used.
It was on the hunting field, in the 1880s. A lady rider
jumped a stone wall and her horse cut its leg badly, sever-
ing an artery. Several men pulled up to help, but decided
the horse would bleed to death before it could be taken to
a vet. Just then an old blind man appeared, led by a girl.
He went straight up to the horse, and holding the lip of
the cut together, murmured something, which appeared
to be repeated three times. To everyone's amazement the
blood ceased to flow. The old man patted the horse's neck

and said, 'He'll do now'; but that it would require five stitches in the cut. Every man there put his hand in his pocket to reward the blind man, but the girl said hastily that he would never take any reward for his help. The old man agreed, adding that the gift would leave him if he did so. The horse *did* require five stitches, and eventually quite recovered.

I have been told three versions of the blood-staunching charm, one of which the old man may have used.

'In our Lord's grave grew three flowers : one was Youth,
The second Virtue, and the third was Truth.
May the blood stop, in the name of Father, Son and
    Holy Ghost.'

This was accompanied by the sign of the cross, and often followed by a triple 'Amen'.

Or :

'Our Lord was born in Bethlehem,
Baptised in Jordan;
There He digged a well
And turned the water against the hill,
So shall this blood stand still.'

Or :

Three Virgins came over Jordan's land,
Each with a bloody knife in her hand;
Stem, blood, stem ! – Letherly stand !
Bloody nose (or mouth – or what) in God's name, mend !'

This was for haemorrhage, bleeding from wounds, etc.

A very old belief was associated with blood-staunching. It was affirmed that should the blood-stauncher cross running water on his way home after a cure, the blood would start to flow once again. It is said the curer often went miles out of his usual way home to prevent this happening.

Nor were these cures only used for human beings. I have been told of a cow which was treated by an old woman for 'udder-ill'. She passed her hand over the affected parts murmuring:

'This cow has udder-ill. It might come from the sun;
It might come from the moon; it might come from the stars;
It might come from the earth. Unto the earth it shall return!'

Then she blew on the place to drive away the 'evil thing' – the old farmer[25] declared that the next day his cow gave a bucket of milk.

In other cases animals were used to assist in cures. It was said that if a child was passed over the back and under the belly of a donkey three times, this would cure whooping cough. For a boy you used a jack donkey and for a girl a jenny, and a few hairs from the cross on the donkey's back were made into a sandwich (chopped) and eaten by the sufferer.

An even more unusual cure for whooping cough was told me by a health visitor, Miss R. Maundrell of Great Bedwyn, in 1973. I had heard of the cure before, but not of a mother actually using it. Nine mice were caught, skinned and roasted, and the child was given three mice to eat on three consecutive days. And, believe it or not, it cured the child.

[25] Mr. Thomas Hawkins, born in Aldbourne.

This Wiltshire charm against toothache[26] was discovered in the Pewsey parish by the then rector, Canon Bouverie.

> 'As Peter sat on a murbal stwone,
> At the geate of Jerusalem,
> The Lord he said to Peter, "Peter,
> What aileth thee?" "Lord, I am
> Trubaled with the toothache."
> "Arise thou up, and follow Me,
> Thou shalt be cured of thy pain,
> And not only thou, but everyone
> That carry these few lines for My seake." '

Canon Bouverie added that his informant believed it 'comes out of the Bible somewhere'.

A Charm to Extract a Thorn :

> 'Happy man that Christ was born !
> He was crownèd with a thorn ;
> He was piercèd through the skin,
> For to let the poison in ;
> But His five wounds, so they say,
> Closed before He passed away.
> In with healing, out with thorn,
> Happy man that Christ was born !'

A Rat Remover :

> 'I order all Rattons that be in this house,
> All mannere of Rattons and eke of Mouse,
> By the grace of Mary, cleane,
> Go hence, Rattons ! and be no more seene.
> And by Him who Mary bore aboute,
> Let NO Ratton stay ! within or withoute,
> And by the Holy Ghost of grace,

[26] Ted Kimber, of Pewsey, recommended a 'twin' hazel nut, carried in the pocket. It worked for me.

That all Rattons leave this place !
By the Father and the Son,
I bid all Rattons to be Gone.'

A Ringworm Charm :[27] On three successive mornings take some ashes between forefinger and thumb and before taking any food, hold to the part affected, saying :

'Ringworm, ringworm red !
Never mayst thou spread or speed.
But aye grow less and less,
And die away among the ase.'[28]

BEAUTY AIDS

*'I've paints and I've perfumes for those who may choose
   them,
Young ladies, I presume you never use them.
The bloom on your cheek is Nature's own painting,
But buy a little toy from poor Rose of Lucerne.'*[29]

Hand Cream : Take four ounces of lanolin, one ounce of white petroleum jelly, one ounce of almond or olive oil, and one ounce of rosewater. Put the lanolin and jelly in a basin, beat well to a cream, adding gradually the oil, beating well all the time. Lastly, add the rosewater, a little at a time. Continue beating until all is mixed together and leave overnight. Next day, beat up again, then pot it.

Nourishing Cream : Take one ounce of white wax, one ounce of spermaceti, five ounces of almond oil, four ounces of rosewater and a few drops of scent. Melt the white wax

[27] Miss Hughes, Bromham.
[28] sc. ashes.
[29] My grandfather, born 1830, said his nurse sang this to him when he was a baby.

and spermaceti in an enamel pan over a slow heat. Then add the almond oil, stirring continuously, then the rosewater drop by drop. Remove from the heat and add the perfume. Stir from time to time until it cools, put into pots and screw down. This will make ten ounces.

New-mown Hay Scent (used mostly by gentlemen) is obtained from a mixture of forty minims of oil of bergamot, forty minims of rose geranium, one ounce of tincture of benzoin, one ounce of essence of musk, one ounce of spirit, and four ounces of tincture of tonka beans.

Pot Pourri : Mix together one ounce of gum benzoin, one ounce each of angelica root and of cloves, a pinch each of nutmeg and cinnamon, four ounces of iris root, two ounces of oil of geranium (or use scented geranium leaves), slices of thin lemon rind, half an ounce of oil of lavender, two ounces of oil of bergamot. This mixture should then be strewn between layers of dried rose petals, etc.

A Good Pomade : Two ounces each of white wax and palm oil, eight ounces each of olive oil and lard, sixpennyworth of bergamot scent. Mix the first four ingredients over a slow fire and add the scent when cold.

Paste for Chapped Hands : Mix a quarter of a pound of unsalted hog's lard, which has been washed in water and then rosewater, with the yolks of two newlaid eggs and a large spoonful of honey. Add as much fine oatmeal or almond flour as will work it into a paste. This whitens the hands as well as softening them.

'Miss in her Teens' (Mrs. Glasse's Scent) : One quart of spirits of wine, one ounce of essence of bergamot, two drachms of oil of rhodium, half a drachm of tincture of

musk, and half a pint of water are mixed well together
and put into bottles for use.

Honey Nourishing Mask : Mix one fresh egg yolk with
two tablespoonfuls of milk, add half a teaspoonful of honey
and beat this to a mayonnaise consistency. Leave on your
face and neck for ten to fifteen minutes, after which remove with hot water.

This can be preceded by the use of –

Soothing Honey Skin Balm : Mix one dessertspoonful of
honey with three fluid ounces of glycerine and one and a
half fluid ounces of lemon juice. Add two fluid ounces of
rosewater and half a fluid ounce of red lotion. This is used
to clear the skin.

A Hair Shampoo : Beat an egg well, and pour into a
half-pint jug, add a teaspoonful of powdered borax and
the juice of half a lemon, then fill up the jug with warm
soft water. This should be well rubbed into the hair before it gets cold. Rinse *very* well – three times at least.

For the Hands and Face : A dessertspoonful each of
glycerine and lemon juice are mixed well together, and a
teaspoonful of eau de Cologne is added last, and mixed in.

Lip Salve : Mix one ounce of olive oil, half an ounce of
spermaceti, quarter of an ounce of white wax together.

A Hair Wash : Put two ounces of glycerine and a teaspoonful of borax into a pint bottle, and fill up with rosemary water.

For the Hair : Steep one pound of rosemary leaves in
boiling water and let them remain standing for twelve
hours. Strain and add to the liquid half an ounce of
Jamaica rum. *Or* : Take one ounce of solution of ammonia, one ounce of oil of almonds, two ounces of spirits

of rosemary and four ounces of honey water. Mix very well and bottle. Apply night and morning to the hair.

Rosemary Pomatum: Strip from the stem a double handful of freshly gathered rosemary. Boil in a tin or copper vessel with half a pound of common soft pomatum, or hog's lard, until reduced to about three or four ounces. Strain it off, and keep it in the usual way. All rosemary remedies are for dark hair – *not* for blonde.

III

FARMER'S LORE

'Let this be held the farmer's creed,
Your land sow with the best of seed,
Let it not dung or dressing need,
Enclose and hedge it with all speed,
And you will soon be rich indeed,
            God speed the plough.'

PLOUGHING

It used to be a tradition in Wiltshire to bring a plough
into the parish church on Plough Sunday, the first Sunday
after Twelfth Night (6th January). In the service which

followed the priest blessed the plough, the farmer and his
farm workers, for the coming year. This service is still
held in Salisbury Cathedral, and also in Pewsey Church,
when the plough is attended by members of the Young
Farmers' Club. The traditional 'Blessing of the Plough' in
the Salisbury Diocese ran :

> 'God speed the plough :
>   the plough and the ploughman,
>   the farm and the farmer,
>   machine and beast and man,
> God speed the plough :
>   the beam and the mouldboard,
>   the slade and the sidecap,
>   the share and the coulters,
> God speed the plough :
>   in fair weather or foul,
>   in success or disappointment,
>   in rains and wind, or in frost and sunshine,
> God speed the plough.'

The Monday after Plough Sunday was Plough Monday,
when the farm men carried the plough round the parish,
stopping at every sizable house, where they expected to
receive refreshment and a donation of money. If this was
not forthcoming the plough was used to 'plough up the
scraper' (and the front garden); so no doubt they generally
got their tip. In some places this money was used for
'plough lights' – a light kept burning all the year in the
church. While it was alight it meant bright times ahead.

Strangely enough, there seem few wise sayings relating
to ploughing. The only ones I can recall are these, about
the tilling of new land :

'Copper is under heather
Silver under gorse,
But gold is under bracken.'

'He that by the plough would thrive
Himself must either hold or drive.'

'Plough deep, while sluggards sleep.'

ANIMALS ON THE FARM

Ashwood sticks were preferred by herdsmen to any other as they were thought to protect the cattle from witchcraft : a beast struck with one would not be harmed. The ash was, popularly, a tree of re-birth; ruptured children were passed through cleft pollard ashes before sunrise as a cure for rupture.

A stable lantern must never be put on a table, but hung from a nail or hook; otherwise, so a Wiltshireman told me, a cow might slip her calf.

'Beastings', the first milk of a cow after calving, brought good luck if sent as a gift to a neighbour, but the bottle which held this must be returned unwashed – otherwise the new-born calf would die, or the cow's milk fail. This also applied to a plate which held a gift of pigmeat, or pig's liver, etc.

To put a hand on a calf's back was most unlucky – the animal so treated would become ill or meet with an accident.

An old notebook of 1859 records that 'a child who sucks a white cow's milk will thrive better'. (Is this a bit of folklore passed down from the white-cow aspect of the British barley-goddess?) But in my young days a red cow's milk was said to be superior to any other. If your milk pan boiled over and the milk fell in the fire, you had immediately to throw salt on the same place, or the cow who gave the milk would suffer from an ulcerated udder.

It was very unlucky to leave a knife on the farm house table overnight – some farm animal would die during the night, and the knife be required to flay it.

It was thought if a billy goat grazed with the herd of cows this prevented *Brucella abortus*. If any ergot was present the billy goat could eat it in small amounts without any harm to himself. Some farmers ran a donkey with the herd, also to prevent contagious abortion. A billy goat was also credited with the ability to prevent ringworm in the cattle with whom he consorted.

An old cattle dealer of Pewsey Vale[1] would never try a second time with an animal which did not enter the waggon – he said something was sure to go wrong if he insisted.

To meet a loaded haycart was lucky, particularly so if drawn by a white horse; if you wished on seeing it, the wish would come true; but the cart had to be coming towards you. If you saw the back of the cart first it was unlucky. You had to look away and not watch it out of sight.

Your field gates had always to be hung to open out of a field – your prosperity would thus expand. A gate opening inwards meant letting adversity in among your stock.

It was thought to be very unlucky to receive any offer of money for your own working dog. The cattle or sheep-dog puppy which sucked the bitch's hind teats would 'keep

<hr />

[1] The late Walter Rawlings.

behind' when it started working. (The hind teats are most productive – a well-fed pup will train more easily.)

One old widespread tradition was that cattle turn to the east on Christmas Eve and kneel in adoration of the Christ Child. In some parts apparently only the three-year-old oxen were thought to kneel, but elsewhere it was those of the age of seven who did so – because that was the age of the oxen in the stable at Bethlehem. In some places cattle were even believed to acquire the gift of speech on Christmas Eve. It was, however, dangerous for any human being to listen to their talk. Whoever did would meet with misfortune, or perhaps hear them speaking of his own death. If so, he would certainly die on the day named, for at that holy season the animals had fore-knowledge, and knew what would occur during the coming year.

Farm animals must not be castrated when the moon is declining, nor should pigs be killed then, or they will not take the salt. Monday (the moon's day) was said to be the luckiest day for pig-killing. 'We don't kill a pig every day' – when we do, and after its hair is scraped off, six small rings are visible, about the size of a pea, and in colour as if burnt or branded on, on the inside of each foreleg, and disposed curvilinearly. It was said by old country folk that these marks were caused by the pressure of the Devil's fingers when he entered the herd of swine which immediately ran violently into the sea (St. Mark VII and St. Luke VIII, 22). It is said pigs can smell wind coming : if they squeal and run about in their sty, we are likely to have windy weather.

The shepherd was king of the old-time farm workers,

and his sheep took precedence over all other animals – the best hay was always for the lambing ewes. A shepherd never allowed his lambs to be counted before lambing time was over; it was unlucky to do so. He would tell enquirers : 'So many singles and so many doubles – I'm not sure.' And old George Frankling once told me, 'The best shepherd that ever ran can't tell if a ewe goes twenty weeks or twenty-one.'

I am told that sheep bells (like horse brasses, which were the property of the carter, not the farmer) belonged to the shepherd.[2] At his death they were often buried with him, or buried in the ground by his family; this accounts for the very few sheep bells to be found today. The bells used to be heard ringing over the downs; twenty or twenty-one sheep bells made a 'set' and their clear notes were obtained by brass or copper hammered into the iron.

It was said that if you saw the first lambs of the year with their heads towards you, you would have good luck that year : if their tails faced you your luck would be 'clean out'. If you had money in your pocket then, it was a fortunate sign; turn it, and you would not lack cash for twelve months. As to the colour of the lambs, it was unlucky for the first lamb dropped in lambing season to be black – black twins were even more unlucky. White twins are lucky, bringing good fortune to the whole flock.

Shepherds would never dock lambs' tails when the moon was waning – if they did the lamb would die. Lamb tail pie or pudding was considered a very great treat; gifts of the lambs' tails were sent to neighbours each May. On the actual shearing of the sheep it was said, 'You may begin

[2] From Mr. A. Ingram, R.S.P.C.A., Devizes.

to shear your sheep when the elder blossoms peep'; and 'Shear sheep in May and you shear them all away; Shear them in June and you'll come home in another tune.'

In the old days a shepherd was often buried with a piece of lamb's wool between his fingers – to explain why, as a shepherd, he had often been unable to attend church service because of his lambing ewes. Some old verses ran :

> 'Over the downs at lambing time
> The bells of a Sunday call;
> Whether or no I must bide from church
> With my ewes and the lambs and all.
> Fine folk passing shake their heads,
> Good folk's kind hearts grieve,
> I'd like to be doing my bit of praise
> If my ewes would give me leave.
> But He that took on Him shepherd's job
> Still walks with my flock and me,
> Every Sunday at lambing time
> I can say my prayer at His knee.
> And when my time comes place in my hand
> A lock of wool from my sheep –
> (Bury me where the down shall watch
> Mother-like o'er my sleep) –
> And when I come to the Gate of Heaven
> Peter will not refuse
> To let me in, though I stayed from church
> Because of my lambing ewes.'

An old friend of my grandfather, a farmer for more than fifty years, died at harvest time, and his grave was lined with corn from his own fields. He took his last journey thither in his best waggon, drawn by his beautiful cart-horses, bedecked with all their horse brasses and attended by his old carters.

HORSE TALES

'Ride a-cock horse to Banbury Cross
To see a fair lady ride on a white horse.'

Stories and legends regarding horses are many in Wiltshire. This, the longest-inhabited part of Britain, is the land of white horses on our chalky hillsides. Admittedly, only one of these – that on Bratton Down (though more generally called the Westbury White Horse) – is of great age : it is supposed to have been cut by King Alfred to commemorate his victory over the Danes at the Battle of Ethandun, about 878 A.D. Unfortunately it was remodelled in 1778 and the old horse lost. The earlier horse is said to have been a rather dachshund-like animal, with long heavy body and short shapeless legs. Both ears were shown, but only one eye, placed under the left ear ! The tail curved upward and had a forked tip, and the creature wore a saddlecloth decorated with crescents. Plenderleath thinks a crescent may also have once been over the tail and that this horse may be contemporary with the Uffington horse.

There is a record in an old poem of a small mettlesome mare – 'the Night Mare'. She is described as not more than thirteen hands high, cream-coloured, with a long head, and flowing mane and tail. Around her neck hangs a shining poitrel (a little moon, a thin disc of Wicklow gold cut in crescent shape, the horns expanded), fastened together behind her neck with a braid of scarlet and white linen. Her speed was wonderful – pity those poor hag-ridden horses found at cockcrow in the stables, nearly foundered, who had to keep up with her. An old charm against the Night Mare, probably fourteenth century, ran :

'Tha mon o' might, he rade o' nicht
Wi' neider swerd ne ferde ne licht,
He socht tha Mare, he found tha Mare,
He bond tha Mare wi' her ain hare,
And gared her swar by midder-nicht,
She wolde nae mair rid o' nicht,
Whar aince he rade, that mon o'nicht.'

The present chalk horse at Bratton is 182 ft. long and
108 ft. high. The other white horses of Wiltshire are the
Alton Barnes horse, cut in 1868, and about 162 ft. long;
the Broad Town horse, cut in 1864; the Cherhill horse, cut
in 1780, and said to be visible for at least thirty miles; the
Hackpen horse, cut in 1838; the Marlborough horse, cut
in 1804; and newest of all, the Pewsey horse, replacing an
old horse cut in 1785 and cut in 1937 to commemorate
King George VI's coronation. There are several other
'lost' horses : 'Snobs' Horse' at Devizes, cut by local shoe-
makers, and one at Rockley; and a small 'donkey' is still
partly visible on Tan Hill, though the legs have become
quite overgrown. The shepherds call this 'Donkey Hill'
and one told me he had 'eaten bread and cheese on its
back scores o' times'. This pony or donkey is 75 ft. from
nose to tail, which stretches down much like that of the
Uffington horse, and its head is very large. The strangest
part of this is that in the 'valley' between Tan Hill and
Rybury Camp stands a miniature stone circle of nine up-
right sarsen stones about four feet in height, in the centre
of which lies a prostrate stone, about the length of a man.
A pathway leads up to the 'donkey' from the circle. In the
Anglo-Saxon Charter mention is made of the 'Anan stones'
as one of the boundary marks between the parishes of All

Cannings and Stanton. Could these be the same stones?

Old John Green, who was born in All Cannings on 5th August 1857 – 'day afore Tan Hill Fair' – told me in 1940 that when the white horse on the hill heard All Cannings' church clock 'hit' midnight, it came down to the dewpond above Cannings Cross to drink. Indeed, the old man added that one night the horse was so thirsty it drank the pond dry – in spite of the fact that a dewpond is said never to dry up. Chris Merritt and other worthies of the village claim the horse is sometimes seen at the top end of the village still. Maybe it accompanies 'the little man in the red hat' on his perambulations?[3]

An archaeologist friend is sure that these recent chalk horses replace very much older figures, cut to surround the great Avebury Circle in honour of the Goddess Estonia. The Rev. W. L. Bowles, writing in 1828, mentions a British trackway which led from Marden (where was a Celtic mound – now demolished – like the one at Marlborough) in a straight line to Tan Hill, and so to Avebury. He suggests that the whole assembly, headed by the priests, may have proceeded along this and that Tan Hill Fair was the remains of this annual assembly.

Tan Hill is the highest peak in the ridge of hills which runs from Devizes to Marlborough. Along the north side lies the deep prehistoric ditch, the Wansdyke (40 ft. deep behind Tan Hill, where it overlooks Avebury). To the south lies Rybury Camp and the site of a prehistoric village. The highest peak is marked on an old map in Devizes Museum as 'Devil's Church' – one wonders why?

[3] See my *Ghosts & Legends of the Wiltshire Countryside*, p. 33.

Tacitus writes that the Belgae had a celebrated temple bearing the name Tan Fana : was some sort of religious assembly, or some hill altar, on Tan Hill in the old days?

Until 1933 Tan Hill Fair, a fair for sheep and horses, had been held at the top of this hill since time immemorial. Only twice had it been missed. The first time is to be seen in the Chamberlain's account for Devizes in 1637, which states : 'The sum of £2 10s. was by Mr. Mayor's appointment paid to Captain Nicholas, as an indemnity for the not keeping Tan Hill Fair, which was interdicted this year in order for the not dispersing of the plague.' The second time was within living memory, in 1914, when England went off the gold standard when the First World War began. It was said that the dealers, unable to obtain supplies of paper money, stayed away, though the hurdles were put up for sheep pens.[4]

The Fair was a general holiday for all the district, as well as a busy sheep and horse fair. At one time there were even roundabouts there. Broad beans, boiled on the spot in water from the dewpond, sold at 'a penny a perch' (as many as could be 'stabbed' by a steel three-pronged fork). About tea time the farmers and dealers departed and then the country folk enjoyed themselves. Indeed, so rowdy did it often become that 'decent girls were gated on that day' – or so I was told.

Strange scraps of tales remain – of the bonfire, for instance, with whispers of a black cock being burnt there. Certainly the ash from the fire was saved; it was, amongst other things, considered a cure for scour in calves

[4] Mr. Frank Cowdrey, All Cannings.

(dysentery) and a good fertiliser for plants. The word 'Tan' itself is said to signify fire; and the white chalk 'scar' down the side of the hill is said to have been made by the Devil's spade.

Tan Hill, being within the parish of All Cannings, is part of the Stadfold Hundred (the fold of the stud), together with Erchfont, Etchilhampton, Allington, Chirton and Stert. Etchilhampton Hill was said to have been the meeting place of this hundred, and Mr. T. C. Lethbridge suggests the name derives from 'the hill or town of the horse'. The old Celtic word *Eachanaidh* meant 'people of the horse' and from this word the ridgeway which runs along below the Uffington White Horse, Icknield Way, is thought to have derived. Erchfont (now written Urchfont) could have been the font – or spring – of the horses. So this corner of Wiltshire may have been the Horse Folk's quiet valley – Pewsey Vale – where the chariot horses were bred.

Old carters would take 'hag stones' (stones which had a natural hole right through them) and hang them on a string, like a necklace, in the stable. This was to protect the horses from spells or disease, or to keep them safe from witches riding them. If the stable door had a key a hag stone was often tied to the ring (this also often applied to a house key), as the combination of iron and stone was believed to provide the most strongly protective charm of any. The same sort of hag stone was often tied to a bed post to guard the occupants of the bed from nightmare.

Different places had their own version of a 'lucky horse'. In one place it would be a horse with one foreleg and one hindleg white-stockinged. A piebald horse was lucky to meet, but a skewbald not lucky. If you met a white horse, you spat and made a wish. Unmarried girls would count the white horses they saw until they numbered a hundred, then the first man with whom they then shook hands, they expected they would marry. My aunt was one person who counted the horses and married the man.

It was said to be very unlucky for a woman to be present when a mare was giving birth to her foal. A brood mare often wore 'a pelican in her piety' horse brass (this showed the bird feeding her brood with blood drawn from her breast); while peacocks (sacred to Hera, the goddess of fertility) were thought to bring luck to a mare in foal. A mare in foal was never put to draw a waggon which was being used to carry a coffin to the church, for if this was allowed, she, or her foal, or both, would die.

One charm connected with the horse is still in use today – the horseshoe. It is still seen nailed over house doors, and even made into knockers. It is said Nelson had a horseshoe nailed to the mast of the *Victory*. For centuries it has been considered a luck-bringer and a protective amulet, partly because it was made of iron, and partly because of its shape, which suggested the new moon. Old blacksmiths used to claim, too, that the old handwrought horseshoe nails – the best shoes and nails were said to be those cast from old ones – had magical properties. If a nail was found, it must be kept for luck by the person who found it and would afford protection from all evil influences, particularly from ghosts.[5]

Some old horsemen appeared to possess strange powers over horses. They could stop them still where they were

[5] Mr. J. Vyner.

standing, and nothing could then induce the horse to move. The old horsemen were very secretive about the source of this power, but it is thought it might be partly caused by a horse's very keen sense of smell. A noxious mixture was evolved – I have heard of the powdered dried liver of stoat or rabbit being one ingredient ! – and secretly rubbed on to some part of the horse, maybe while the horsemen pretended to feel its fetlock. This caused the animal to remain stock still, refusing to advance nearer the dreadful odour. When the horseman wished to release the horse, he would smear his hand with milk and vinegar which would mask the smell and the horse would move forward when told. There was also a tale that a horseman must be possessed of a frog-bone, if he wished to have this magical power over horses. A dead frog or toad was placed in an anthill where the ants would eat all the body, leaving only the skeleton, which was then thrown into a running stream on the night of the full moon. It was said one bone would separate from the rest and float against the running tide : this was the magic-bone and must be caught before it sank. It would seem to have been a mixed blessing to own this magic bone, however, and the owner often 'paid' for having such a prize.

These old horsemen were said to form a Horsemen's Society, men who worked amongst horses – carters, plough-men, grooms, blacksmiths, and horse leaders; but farmers and their sons were excluded. It was said their initiation took place in the blacksmith's smithy, grouped around the anvil, at twelve midnight. Twelve horsemen and the leader, who was said to wear stag's horns on his head at the ceremony, received a new member, who had to swear

'to hele,[6] conceal and never reveal' any of the secrets of the
Horseman's Society. Alas, the great horses and their horsemen have nearly disappeared from our farms today, and
the old carters do not keep a brown paper parcel of clipped
'she' yew under their beds for a year or more before adding
a little to the horse's bait to make his coat shine and
generally improve his appearance before any special occasion. Another herb used for its stimulative properties was
the 'spignel meum',[7] or 'baldmoney', the feathery leaves of
which were given to horses before sending them to a show
or a fair. They were *never* to be given to a mare. Chopped
walnut leaves were said to be good for worming horses;
and for this some carters also used horse-hair, cut up small
and mixed into the feed.

Marchwort put into drinking troughs was said to keep
animals healthy, but this would only work if the herb was
picked with the left hand, without looking back. Gervaise
Markham, a noted authority on farriery in the seventeenth
century, prescribed balls made from garlic, liquorice and
aniseed for horses suffering from the nightmare. Sores on
horses, or indeed on any domestic animal, were said to be
cured by gathering red thistles before daybreak and put-
ting one in each corner of the compass, with a stone in the
middle.

To call – or as they put it, draw – a horse to the horseman (generally used for young colts or vicious older
horses), most of the old horsemen had a secret mixture

[6] A similar oath was taken by pre-Christian priests. The word 'hele'
is obscure : it could mean 'to cover', as when a gardener 'heels' in a
plant – or from Anglo-Saxon *halig*, meaning 'holy'.
[7] This herb has a strong pleasant aromatic scent and very small
greenish-yellow flowers which appear in June.

which they jealously guarded. One such was a mixture of oil of origanum, oil of rosemary, oil of cinnamon, and oil of fennel; these 'drawing oils' were either put on the horseman's person or else the horse was given lumps of sugar with a few drops of the oil on them. This sort of oil was also used by gamekeepers and by poachers to attract game birds, and they also used an oil of rhodium for the same purpose. These tricks of jading and drawing a horse (dramatically stopping a horse and forcing it to remain still was called 'jading', while calling a horse, or quietening an unruly animal was know as 'drawing') were very old indeed. It is said that in 481 A.D. after the Gothic victory, Clovis, king of the Salic Franks, made rich offerings to St. Martin of Tours; but when he wished to redeem his warhorse by the gift of one hundred pieces of gold, the enchanted steed could not move from the stable till the price of his redemption had been doubled. This miracle provoked the king to exclaim, *'Vere, B. Martinus est bonus in auxilio, sed carens in negotio.'* ('Indeed, St. Martin may be a good friend when you're in trouble, but he's an expensive one to do business with.') It is evident that the priests who served St. Martin knew how to jade a horse, and to attribute its state to the Saint's intervention. Christianity was adapting the old pagan beliefs and arts for its own purpose.

These practices were still being used at the beginning of the twentieth century. I was told of a harvest waggon coming up from the field, when the horses suddenly stopped and refused to go any further; they were as fixed as if something was holding them on to the road, until someone fetched one of the old horsemen and he got the team moving again without any trouble – no doubt with a hand covered with milk and vinegar which neutralised the smell of the repellent substance first used.

Small wonder the horsemen setting out on a journey would sometimes mutter :

> 'Matthew, Mark, Luke and John,
> Hold this horse that I ride on,
> Hold him fast, and hold him sure,
> Till I win o'er the misty moor.'

This was a variation of the prayer used by country folk when they went to bed in John Aubrey's day :

> 'Matthew, Mark, Luke and John,
> Bless the bed that I lye on.
> And blessed Guardian Angel keep
> Me safe from danger whilst I sleep.'
> *Lansdowne M.S.* 231

THE BEASTS AND THE BIRDS

'Let us a little permit Nature to take her own way; she better understands her way than we.'
MONTAIGNE – *Essays* : 'Experience'

Many of the beasts and the birds had their legends. The shrew, or harvest mouse, was thought to be an evil omen if met when going on a journey; country folk still believe these mice are unable to cross a path which has been trodden by man – if they attempt it they are 'struck dead'. This is thought to account for those found lying dead upon a path on summer evenings.

If you should see a lone crow perched in your path, this is a sign, they say, of wrath (whose?). To see a crow flying

alone is a sign of bad luck; in fact many single birds seem
to be thought the same. My uncle[8] always raised his hat if
he met a jackdaw or crow, and said 'Good morning, Jack'
– a salutation which was said to cancel out the evil. It was
said the magpie would not go into the ark with Noah,
preferring to stay outside and jabber maliciously over
the drowning world; this made it an unlucky bird. Should
a magpie perch on a roof it was a sure sign the roof was
sound, and a tree so used would be never uprooted even in
a violent gale.

An old rhyme regarding such birds runs :

> 'One for sorrow, two for joy,
> Three for marriage, four a boy
> Six for silver, seven for gold,
> Eight is a secret that's never been told.'

When the cuckoo was heard for the first time that year,
you turned your silver and made a wish.[9] If you were
standing on soft ground you had an easy year ahead, but
if on hard ground you might have hard times.

Should you hear the cuckoo after Old Midsummer Day
(3rd July) it is thought to be a death omen. The traditional
date of the cuckoo's first appearance in various localities
seemed often to be related to the date of the local fair.
In the Devizes area it was said, 'Cuckoo be come to vair',
meaning 20th April, the Devizes spring fair. A child born
on the day the first cuckoo of the year is heard was thought
to be lucky throughout life.

The swallow was considered a lucky bird. It was lucky

[8] J. T. Morgan.
[9] Mr. Harry Skinner, Somerset's Farm, Wootton Rivers.

for the inhabitants of the house should the swallow build
under the eaves, and it was thought the birds protected
the house from thunder and lightning. But should the
swallow desert, this brought ill luck; and to destroy the
swallows' nests was the most unlucky thing anyone could
do.[10] The ill luck was thought to follow even into the next
generation.

Yet my grandmother had a legend about the swallow
which did not portray the bird in such a favourable light.
She said that when the Virgin Mary lived in Nazareth she
had a serving-maid who was a thief. One day the girl stole
a pair of scissors and a ball of red silk from Mary Mother's
sewing basket. When accused, she denied it; whereupon
the Virgin struck her with her hand and she was turned
into a swallow, the scissors being the bird's long tail and
the red ball of silk which she had put in the bosom of her
dress being the red feathers at the swallow's throat. She
was doomed forever to fly between earth and sky and never
may she alight on a green bough. And her song was,

> ' "You stole my silk, my scissors too"
> The Virgin said; I did not rue
> But swore I'd not, by salt and bread,
> And brought this doom on my own head.'

Strangely enough, though the toad is so closely associated with witchcraft and magic, it was considered lucky
to meet a toad. Country folk say to kill a toad brings rain
and may cause a storm. Mrs. Jack Maslen of All Cannings
who accidently did kill one told me she would rather have
lost £5.

[10] H. J. Wiltshire, Rustic Farm, All Cannings.

The toad figures in many witch brews, and in some horrible cures also. One very malign tale was of one way to become a witch : the woman attended the Communion service, and retained the consecrated bread in her mouth until she came out of the church. Here she would be met by a toad, when she must spit out the bread, which the toad would eat – this toad, of course, was considered to be the Devil himself.

Moles' feet were often carried as a charm against cramp. If this was in the arms, the forefeet were used, and if in the legs the hind feet. To carry the wrong set was thought to increase the trouble rather than aid it.

For an owl to hoot continually around the village was said to mean any pregnant woman therein would have a daughter; or some girl was about to lose virginity.

It was a sign of fine weather if bats came out early in the evening, and flew about as if playing; but it was said to be a death omen if bats flew three times around the house. The bat was another creature into which witches were said to transform themselves, as too was the fox. It was lucky to meet a single fox, but unlucky to meet several together. Some people say anyone bitten by a fox is marked for death within seven years; but I can refute that – my grandfather was bitten in the 1880s and died in 1921. Foxes are said to get rid of fleas by taking a piece of sheep's wool in their mouth, and then immersing in a stream with only the tip of the nose – and the tuft of wool – above water; the fleas take refuge on the wool, the fox drops it into the water, and emerges free of its pests. Scores of countryfolk swear they have seen this happen.

Then there is the hedgehog, which country folk often call the 'agiboar' (hedge boar) or 'vuzpig' (furzepig). Perhaps it was cooked in olden days, and tasted like pork, as a gipsy once told me; she wrapped the hedgehog in clay, and put it thus into the heart of her fire; when it was cooked, the clay was peeled off, taking the hedgehog's spines away, too.

The old rhyme about the spider will be familiar :

'If you wish to live and thrive, let a spider run alive.'

It is said the spider wove her web across the mouth of a cave in which the Holy Family hid on their journey to Egypt. The soldiers sent by Herod saw the web and did not trouble to search the cave.

Should a spider, particularly the midget 'money' spider, descend from the ceiling upon your head, it should at once be put into your pocket, for it brings you the promise of money to come.

It is also still a general belief that snakes cannot live within the Avebury Circle. I often wonder if there may be a lost legend about this belief, since carved on the Saxon font in Avebury Church is a bishop, clad in cape and mitre and holding his crosier, with which he is spearing a creature – snake, scorpion or even maybe a dragon.

The adder, it was thought, would be always killed by a single blow from an ash stick (the ash protected the stick's bearer from snake bites), but another superstition has it that no snake, however maimed, dies before sundown. And a snake seen near the farmhouse was very unlucky and often foretold a death in the farmer's family.

WEATHER PREDICTIONS

'When it is evening, ye say, "It will be fair weather;
for the sky is red." And in the morning, "It will be foul
weather today, for the sky is red and lowring." '

Matthew XV, 2-3

Even in biblical days men tried to foretell the weather, and
many old country weather beliefs are very ancient indeed.
One that I believe is particularly Wiltshire in origin[11] is the
one which says the first twelve days of any year foretell
what the weather will be for the coming twelve months. I
have found that as a rough estimate it is often a good guide.

Another very common belief is that 'if the wind is in the
east on Candlemas Day, there it will stop till the second of
May.' Candlemas was a well-known weather presignifica-
tion : many people believed if the sun shone before noon
on that day, winter was only half gone. Indeed, another
saying ran : 'A farmer should have still, on Candlemas
Day, half his litter (straw) and half his hay.'[12] There was
some discussion as to the date of Candlemas : the Church
said 2nd February while Devizes Candlemas Fair was held
on 14th February. This no doubt arose when the calendar
was put forward in the seventeenth century, and so lost
eleven days.

Old John Green, of All Cannings, born 1857, told me
these sayings :

'March dust be worth a guinea a hounch.'

'A cold and dry March never yet begged his bread', but
'a wet and warm March do make a sad harvest.'

[11] Joe Woodruff, All Cannings.
[12] Joe Pierce, thatcher, of Wilcot.

'Where the wind be on March 21st, there it will bide till old May be out.' (That is on 11th June.)

'You should see one ear o' corn afore old May be out – if so be as you do look in the right place.'

He also said, 'A wet May be the making o' everything.'

Another old man of about the same age, John Cook of All Cannings, told me, 'Barley ears always turn to face north.' (The north was once supposed to be the Devil's quarter – the north door of a church was only opened to allow the Devil to escape after a baptism.) He also said it was always windy for barley harvest: God knocked off ears for the poor.

He had another odd saying, too : 'If it rains whilst the sun is shining, the Devil is beating his grandmother – he is laughing whilst she cries.'

A very common belief in Wiltshire ran, 'As many mists in March you see, so many frosts in May will be' – and I have often found this to be true. They also say, 'In the middle of May comes the tail of winter.' 'Blackthorn winter' was a cold spell of about three weeks whilst the blackthorn blossom was out in flower.

Some of the rhymes are very old :

'The rainbow in th' marnin' gies the shepherd warnin'
To car' his girt cwoat on his back;
Rainbow at night be shepherd's delight,
For there no girt cwoat will be lack.'

And another :

'When the oak's before the ash,
There you'll only get a splash;
If the ash precedes the oak,
Then you may expect a soak.'

And also :

'If the oak leaves before the ash, there will be fine weather for harvest.'

My grandmother used to tell me if it rained on 22nd July, St. Mary Magdalen was washing her kerchief in readiness for the fair on the feast day of her cousin, St. James the Great, on 25th July. She also used to quote :

> 'If our Lord falls in our Lady's lap,
> England will meet with a great mishap.'

This was saying that if either Good Friday or Easter Sunday falls on 25th March (Lady Day) some national disaster will follow within twelve months. It is worth noting in this context that in 1910 Good Friday fell on 25th March, and the following May King Edward VII died after a short illness; and in 1951 Easter Sunday fell on the same ominous date, and a little less than eleven months later King George VI died.

Though it was said that to kill a black slug was a sure way to bring rain within twenty-four hours, it was considered so unlucky that in the severest drought no one would venture to do so.

Molehills were considered to foretell the weather – very deep molehills (2½ ft. or so) predicted a hard winter, and should you see new earth thrown up in a frost it meant warmer weather to come.

Mr. Harry Skinner, a farmer of Wootton Rivers, on the border of Savernake Forest, once told me should a stag rise with dry horns on Holy Rood Day (4th September)[13] it will

[13] Wilcot church was dedicated to the Holy Cross; this is not far from Wootton Rivers.

be a fine autumn; if the horns are wet, so will the autumn be.

All the corn sowings had rules to guide their time.

'Drunk or sober, sow your wheat in October.'

'Who in Februeer sows oats
Gets both gold and groats' – (a silver fourpenny piece).

'When the blackthorn blossoms white
Sow your barley day and night.'

Another of Mr. Skinner's sayings was, 'Frost in November enough to bear a duck, Naught else all the year excepting slush and muck'; while another prophecy ran, 'If ducks do swim at Hallantide (11th November) at Christmas they will slide.' At this time of year it is also said, 'Clear morn – frost soon.' A little later on, we are told, 'A green Christmas, a fat churchyard' – inferring mild weather is not healthy at that time of year.

Shepherds on Salisbury Plain had a saying :

'When dotterels first appear – frost is near;
But when the dotterels go – look for snow.'

Black snails across the path, donkeys wagging their heads, cats sneezing and wiping their mouths with their paws, crickets chirping – all are said to be signs of rain. If the cats go over both ears, you can expect snow.

And, finally : 'Winter thunder – summer wonder.'

WELLS, SPRINGS AND DEWPONDS

Certain wells and springs have always been thought by country folk to have curative properties – even rainwater at certain times. To obtain these benefits a gift had to be offered – a piece of money, usually silver; a crooked pin, or a needle were often so used. If nothing was given you would hear the Devil laugh from the bottom of the water.

A well at the old vicarage at Keevil was well known for its curative properties, particularly for eye complaints, and old inhabitants used to remember people coming with bottles to carry the water home. Near Luckington, one of the rising places of the Bristol Avon at Brook End, Hancock's Well also had curative properties.

The village of Crudwell had an even more unusual well, the water from which was said to possess the power of turning milk into cream. From this notion John Aubrey derived the name of the village, but other people considered it to be 'Creodan Well' – the well of Cridda, King of Mercia, who was slain in the neighbourhood in 573 A.D.

Seend has two once well-known chalybeate springs, which in the eighteenth century drew many people there on account of their healing properties. Another less-known mineral spring is at Purton Stoke, said to possess great medicinal properties. Purton was the birthplace of James II's Queen Anne (Hyde) whose father, the famous Lord Clarendon, once lived there in a house now known as College Farm.

Limpley Stoke has an ancient holy well known as Shingle Bell Well, but I have not heard that its water is curative. Westbury has a very ancient spring, Bridewell Springs (in 1341 it was called Bride Welle) and no doubt this was considered a fertility spring.[14]

Mere also has a very old spring or well, called Holewell; though associated with St. Osmund in 1495, its name

[14] Mrs. J. Morrison, Bratton.

does not mean 'holy well', but is said to refer to the 'spring in the hollow'.

At Market Lavington, at the foot of Clyffe Hall hill, on the left-hand side when travelling from Market Lavington, is a very small horse trough with a stone recess above which used to contain a drinking cup chained to it. Mrs. T. Gye, of Market Lavington, was told by her aunt, Mrs. Apps of Calne (brought up in Market Lavington): 'When I was a child people believed that the water from this spring was good for eyesight. An old woman who was growing blind from cataract, which she refused to have treated, used to stand and catch my brother and me as we came home from our governess, with a request to get her a jug of this healing water. It was a red glass jug – I can see it in my imagination now. We hated the job, but I recall we always did it together; I remember one Lent my mother thought it was a good thing for us to do.' This would be about 1890. Mrs. Gye adds, 'I mentioned this trough in a talk at West Lavington W.I. in 1973 and a member told me that this belief was also held by West Lavington people, as recently as thirty years ago, she thought.'

The name of the village of Fovant is said to derive from 'Fobbas Spring', while Urchfont appears as Erches fonte in 1086, which is thought may be 'Eohric's spring' – the spring of the fawn, or the spring of the horse. In any case, it is said to be the fount of seven springs and it never runs dry.

When I came to All Cannings in 1938, I heard two village women talking in the village shop and one was recommending the water from a certain local spring for eczema; and I know two springs which were thought wonderful for brewing tea, so much so that one man would walk a mile to bring back a bottleful for this purpose. It was also said to improve the making of beer and home-made wine.

Springs were used in divination and for the granting of wishes. The person cupped the water with his hands and drank three times; what water remained was thrown on a stone, the wish expressed, and the gift to the spring given. To discover if a sick person would get better, a wooden dish was carried to the water and gently put on it to float; if the bowl turned to the south, the patient would recover; if otherwise, not. To take water to a sick person, it was said the water must be drawn in a vessel which on no account must touch the ground; the person drawing it must turn himself round 'with the sun' and throw some of the water over his left shoulder, then carry it to the sick person, 'salute no one by the way' and leave a piece of silver in the well or spring.

Another way was to take the water in 'a quick cow's horn' (a horn taken from a live cow) and spill it on the ground three times; this must be done before the sun rises or immediately after it has set. Again, you gave a silver coin, except in cases of epilepsy, when a cock or hen was the offering. To bathe in such water on the first Sunday in May was considered an infallible cure for almost any disease – sore eyes, sprains, and the like.

There is a 'wishing well' on Roundway Down called Mother Anstey's Well,[15] a pilgrim's well in the grounds of Bradenstoke (Clack) Abbey, and a pond with a history at Neston, near Corsham. It is known as Whores' Pool and

[15] Miss Janet Butcher.

in the Middle Ages it boasted a ducking stool for 'scolding
wives and women of ill-repute'. It is apparently in poor
condition today.

At the Devil's Den, near Marlborough, a tradition tells
if a person pours water into the natural cup-shaped cavi-
ties on the top stone at midnight it will always be found to
to be gone in the morning – drunk by the Devil.

On many of the Wiltshire Downs we can still find a
dewpond. The one on Milk Hill is known as Oxenmere,
and it is said that the oxen were watered here. On
Martinsell, near Marlborough, the dewpond is known
locally as Sugar Pond, which used to puzzle me when I was
small; but Sugar Hill at Aldbourne is said to have been
'Shuger waie' in 1591 (the robbers' way or path) and this
crosses the Roman road from Cirencester to Silchester, so
that travellers along that road may have been robbed
by those hiding on the 'Shuger waie'. Maybe there was a
robber gang on Martinsell also.

The ancient traditional craft of pond-making up on the
downs was a skilled hereditary calling, which demanded
knowledge, strength and skill, and the family secret of
pond-making was often passed down from father to son for
hundreds of years. One of these families had been involved
in it for over 250 years, though I heard lately that some
people today thought dewponds to be phenomena of
nature.

Many years ago an old dewpond-maker of Wiltshire[16]
described pond-making to an aunt of mine; I was also
there, and later noted down what he had said. This is how
it went :

[16] Mr. A. Smith of Market Lavington.

'You shape your hollow according to the amount of water required; then you beat it down all over with your feet; now you take clay from the hills – not the stuff from the builders – and put six inches of it all over your hollow. Now comes the hard work – puddling – which means glazing the clay to make it impervious to water. This glazing is done by pushing heavy bitles (often made of apple wood) all over the clay until a smooth surface is obtained, and this demands knowledge of the proper moisture and consistency of the clay for puddling, and great strength, accuracy and rhythm in the ramming and beating with the bitle. Two inches of lime comes next, and calls for the adept use of a specialised tool for pressing the new-slaked lime over the surface of the clay. Then comes four inches of straw, shaken on rough, and a trained eye for the right depth is required here; finally, you cover it all with rough local earth, which may be full of clay or chalk – it does not matter. You spread it all over, beat it down with your feet, and with beaters, and very soon there is your pond.'[17]

Some country men declared a dewpond required to be 'started off' with perhaps a barrel of water, after which it would never be found to be dry; omit this 'starter', however, and the pond would remain dry.

It is said the secret of the dewpond lies in the warm straw, which causes condensation on the top of the cold, hard clay. As the water collects, it is retained, and no matter how small the rainfall, there is always two-thirds more water in the pond. And provided no one rams a

[17] Mr. Patrick Gale says there are five dewponds on Temple Farm, Rockley, all lined by sarsen stones, which were shaped by an old flint-knapper, whose forefathers, all flint-knappers, lived in Rockley (near Marlborough).

hole in the clay it is good forever. Such Wiltshire dewponds have been used by country folk, particularly shepherds, from time immemorial.

THE TRUFFLE HUNTERS

I recently looked up my grandmother's old recipe for the stuffing of pheasant. As I turned the yellow pages of the old book containing her treasured recipes, I remembered how her friends – and even relations – were considered honoured to have any of these closely guarded family secrets passed on to them. Nor was Grandma alone in this trait : it was told of another housewife of that day that she carried her recipe book to her bedroom each night, together with the silver basket, and slept with the book and her keys safely tucked beneath her pillow.

In the old recipe book, written with old time flourishes, were the necessary ingredients I was looking for : chopped pork and minced button onions, sausagemeat and sundry herbs, lemon peel and red wine – and truffles. Here was one ingredient I would *not* be able to include.

I wonder how many of our younger generation have tasted – perhaps even heard of – the subterranean fungi considered such a delicacy by our forebears. Wiltshire, with all its chalk downlands, was found most rewarding by the old truffle hunters. There is a legend that the first Wiltshire truffle hunter was a survivor from the Spanish Armada, who was shipwrecked on the Sussex coast; he is said to have settled in a cottage near Stonehenge, and when he died he left his truffle-hunting trained poodles to the farmer who had befriended him.

Sixty or seventy years ago the Wiltshire village of Winterslow was said to have ten professional truffle hunters. The Collins family who lived in Winterslow boasted of one, Eli, who was said to have been the most famous truffler in England.[18] The season for hunting truffles began in November, and ended in February. The fungi were scented out by dogs – often poodles – though I have been told some sows had a 'nose' for the delicacy, too. They were generally to be found under trees – oak trees most often – and the best spot was a plantation of trees between ten and twenty years of age, as these afforded the right degree of sun and shade. Salisbury Plain was said to be a rewarding area.

In Victorian times a truffler could make five shillings a day, which he then considered riches – a farm worker often had only a wage of ten shillings a week. Nowadays it would not pay a man to spend all day hunting for truffles, and maybe the present day folk would have lost the taste for them anyway. One man said truffles were found two to eight inches below hazel or beech trees, and he had sold them for three shillings a pound.

Truffles figure in many old recipes: amongst many modes of cooking they were used as fillings for omelettes, put into meat pies, or stewed in red wine.

[18] He was retained by the Earl of Radnor, who provided his corduroy suits.

IV

HOME AND HOMESTEAD

'Trifles mar tranquility.'
OLD ENGLISH PROVERB

'Alas ! you know the cause too well;
The salt is spilt, to me it fell.
Then to contribute to my loss,
My knife and fork were laid across,
On Friday, too ! the day I dread;
Would I were safe at home, in bed !
Last night (I vow to Heaven 'tis true)
Bounce from the fire a coffin flew;
Next post some fatal news shall tell,
God send my Cornish friends be well !'

GAY – *Fables, Part* I, *Fable* 37

SUPERSTITIONS

If superstition was rife about the countryside, within the homestead it seems to have been even more universal. Some of these sayings and beliefs are undoubtedly very old indeed, and may even reach back to the pre-Roman times. Others, I have a shrewd suspicion, may have been the brainchild of some busy housewife, who hoped thereby to hasten laggard maids or daughters in their tasks – for instance, the belief that when sweeping an upper room the dust collected must be carried out of the house before noon, or very bad luck would attend the sweeper.

A guest chamber was not to be swept until the guest who recently occupied it had been out of the house an hour or more. Otherwise, he or she might have bad luck on the journey, or – another version – be prevented from ever returning to the house. Was this thought up by a worn-out hostess?

It was unlucky for a visitor to put the chair on which he was sitting against the wall of the room; if he did, he would never come to that house again.[1] It was unlucky to break pottery on Good Friday; and to carry a spade on the shoulder through the house was a sure sign that a grave would soon be dug, most probably for someone living in the house.

A well-known belief is that it was unlucky to have three lights in a room, be they candles, lamps or rushlights; and even in 1973 I was astonished when I switched on a third electric light to have a quick 'Do we want three lights?' from a middle-aged man.

[1] Mrs. Smart, Wootton Rivers.

The heart of the home is said to be its fireplace – perhaps that is why no one was allowed to poke another's fire, unless he had known the household for at least seven years. And should your fire be slow to light, or be 'sulky', you were often told your sweetheart or your spouse was annoyed with you.[2]

It was said if an extra place were laid at a meal an unexpected guest would arrive before the meal was over – one of many beliefs around the various meals. Should anyone drop a knife, a male visitor was coming – the size of the knife telling how tall the visitor. If our carving knife fell to the floor my aunt invariably remarked, 'The rector' (a very tall big man), who often then came. A fork dropped foretold a woman visitor, while a spoon meant a foal – or, as some say, a child. And to sharpen a knife after sunset warned that an enemy or a thief would enter your house. Two teaspoons accidentally put into a saucer of a teacup was the sign of a wedding within a year. Should you unintentionally leave the lid off the teapot, or place the kettle spout backward on the fire, a stranger could be expected to call. It was considered unlucky to stir tea in the pot, it caused quarrels; and should two women pour tea from the same brewing, one of them would have a baby within the year, or a member of that woman's family would have a new arrival. The same is said should your apron drop from your waist; while it was thought you could change your luck by turning your apron.[3]

Many old superstitions concerned water and washing. It was very unlucky for two friends to wash their hands in

[2] The late Mrs. E. Butler, East Wick Farm, Wootton Rivers.
[3] Mrs. James, All Cannings.

the same water – they would have a lively quarrel, unless they spat in the bowl; and should you also dry on the same towel you would go begging together. For the house-wife to spill water meant her house would be full of visitors before she could mop it up. Should a new garment be washed for the first time when the moon was new, it would not wear well, and persistent appearance in ironed linen of a diamond-shaped mark (known as 'the coffin') was held to be a death omen; if on a sheet, a death soon on the bed on which it was used; on a tablecloth, a departure from the house, or death of someone sitting at the table.

It was unlucky to wash clothes on New Year's Day:

> 'If you wash on New Year's Day
> You'll wash one of your family away.'

and

> 'Wash blankets in May
> Wash the head of the house away.'[4]

In some places in Wiltshire it was said if washing was done on Good Friday, the water would turn to blood.[5]

The position of a bed in your bedroom was very import-ant: beds should point east and west, never north and south, or you would have nightmares: if this occurred, you had only to tie a hag stone to your bedhead to become immune.

It was unlucky to 'turn' a bed on a Friday or a Sunday – you would have bad dreams all the following week if you did; and 'if you wish your love to wed, turn your bed from foot to head'. Should three people make a bed someone

[4] Miss J. E. H. Cave.
[5] Mrs. Jim Burry.

would die in it before the year was out, and it was unlucky to get out of bed a different side from the one you got in. If you crossed anyone on the staircase, you would not meet them in Heaven, while should you trip or stumble going up the stairs, the person following you would be married within a year.

Baking day was most important in the farmhouse. A cross was placed on all home baked bread (not only on hot cross buns) to keep the Devil away and protect the bread from witches whilst baking. This also applied to home-brewed beer. Only one person should put bread into the oven – if two did so they would quarrel; and it was most unlucky to place a loaf upside down on the table, or to cut a loaf at both ends – for then 'the Devil will fly over the house'. It was equally unlucky to throw any bread on to the fire – 'you will live to be hungry'. To help oneself to the last slice of bread on a plate was also unlucky, though if it were offered, and taken, good luck (often quoted as 'a handsome husband, £1,000 a year, and a park') would follow. To make toast from the point of a knife was very unlucky, as was spinning a knife on the table.

Butter-making day was another busy occupation. It was often hindered by a witch who prevented the butter from 'coming'; to prevent this, salt was thrown on to the fire before commencing to churn butter, or else a silver coin placed in the cream. I have even heard of a red-hot poker being plunged into the cream by a harassed housewife.

Often some herb was used in the making of cheese, differing from farm to farm. Nettle juice was sometimes added to the curd, as it was thought to bring a special flavour to the cheese. Lady's bedstraw was another herb so used : this was also said to add colour to the cheese and some people considered it to be a substitute for rennet. Marigold flowers were used for colouring both butter and cheese in Wiltshire and my grandmother used the water in which carrots had been soaked for colouring pale butter in the winter.[6]

The broom's association with witchcraft will have something to do with the number of superstitions relating to it. The witch's broomstick, on which she was thought to fly to her covens, was made of special materials. It had to have an *ash* handle (to protect the witch from drowning), *birch* twigs to form the brush (because when evil spirits were banished, some of those in the birch tree got entangled in the branches and remained), and *osier,* or *willow,* to bind this on (in honour of Hecate the prototype witch to whom it was dedicated). One of the superstitions was that whenever a woman swept a floor she should sweep the dust inwards, never outwards through the door; if she swept it outwards, it would carry away all the money and good fortune of the family. This is a very old belief, for the story is told of Lady Alice Kyteler[7] sweeping the dust from other people's doors, saying as she went :

> 'To the house of William, my son,
> Hie all the wealth of Kilkenny town.'

It was said if you left a broom in a corner or let it fall in anyone's path, before nightfall you would receive a visit from your greatest enemy. Worse still, if a girl acci-

[6] Mrs. T. Morgan.
[7] A celebrated Irish witch, about 1323.

dentally stepped over a broom handle, it was said she would be a mother before she was a wife.[8] To leave a broom standing outside the door was said to be an invitation for a man to visit the mistress of the house.

Perhaps because they also have association with witchcraft, there are several sayings about cats. A cat born just about Michaelmas was called a 'blackberry cat' and was expected to be extremely mischievous in its youth. Cats born in the month of May would neither catch mice nor rats but would bring snakes and slow-worms into the house. Because of this belief, May kittens were often killed; indeed in an old book of 1859 there is an entry, 'You should drown a May kitten, it is unlucky to keep it.' I had a beautiful tabby cat, Tangle, for over fifteen years; she was May-born and a mighty hunter of mice. As for the old saying (also 1859) 'A May baby is always sickly, you may try, but you'll never rear it' – I am a 'May baby' myself.

If you dropped scissors and they stuck in the floor, you would receive news in a letter; if a needle stuck in the floor – only a letter. The gift of a knife or pair of scissors must be paid for by a small coin or they would cut the friendship. If your ears burned someone was talking about you: 'Left for love, right for spite, but either side is good at night'; or 'Left your lover, right your mother.'

It was very unlucky to meet a 'square-eyed' (cross-eyed) woman when going to market, hunting, or on a journey – you would lose money, have no sport, or meet with trouble.[9] But should your nose itch you would either be kissed, cursed, vexed, would run against a gatepost, or

[8] Mrs. E. Nash, All Cannings.
[9] James Morgan, my great-grandfather.

shake hands with a fool. (My uncle invariably held out his hand if anyone rubbed their nose.)

If your hand itched, the right hand foretold you were to pay out money; if the left hand, you would receive it; but about either hand my grandfather[10] would remark, 'Rub it on wood, sure to come good.' (Touch wood?)

My grandfather would never allow anyone to help another to salt at the table : 'Help you to salt, help you to sorrow.' Of course, everyone knew if salt was accidentally spilt, a pinch of the spilt salt must immediately be thrown over the left shoulder three times (in the direction of the Devil?). If anyone asked for a loan of it, the salt must be given as a gift. Salt was often taken as one of the first things into a new house, and also put over a tooth from a child's first set before casting the tooth into the fire.

When moving into a new house, to enter by the back door for the first time was unlucky, and in the old house a penny was always left, which warded off ill-luck from the outgoing tenant and brought good luck to the new.

The iron cross which was sometimes seen on the walls of old houses, and often said to be put on them to correct a slipping wall, was in the old days a charm to keep lightning away. Old country folk always covered all mirrors with a cloth during a thunderstorm, as well as all spoons, forks, knives and steel knitting needles. Advice to anyone caught in open country during a storm is contained in the old rhyme :

> 'Beware of the oak; it draws the stroke;
> Avoid the ash, it courts the flash;
> Creep under a thorn, it can save you from harm.'

[10] Tom Morgan (born 1830).

Several plants or flowers were supposed to cause thunder and lightning: if you picked poppies from amongst the corn, you would either have a bad headache or there would be thunder and lightning; but poppies on the roof of a building kept lightning away. Bugle was credited with the same power and it also cured wounds. Houseleek growing on your roof was considered as good as a fire insurance, while to pick white campion brought thunder, and, some said, death from lightning.

In the old days, the bells of Malmesbury Abbey were pealed during thunderstorms, so John Aubrey writes in his *Miscellanies*:

'Heretofore in Wiltshire, when it thundered and lightened, they did ring St. Aldhelm's[11] bell at Malmesbury Abbey. The curious do say that the ringing of bells exceedingly disturbs spirits.'

Bells were also thought to protect people from snakes. St. Berin (or Berinus), the Apostle of Wessex, who died in Dorchester in A.D. 650, was said to have been killed by an adder bite. It was said snakes could not live within the sound of the tenor bell of the Abbey church (cast in 1380) which has a Latin inscription invoking the Saint.

VEGETABLE DYES FOR SPINNING

Spinning is a household activity rarely seen today (though we do have a busy spinning-wheel in our village). A couple of hundred years ago it was a feature of practically every

[11] Aldhelm was the seventh-century British Bishop of Sherborne, a kinsman of King Ina.

home. One of my treasures is the first baby-cap of my great-great-grandfather, Christopher Exelby (born 1760). It is of linen, edged with very fine knitted lace, and it is told the linen yarn was spun by his mother (née Christianna Hawkswell). I have no means of telling if the recipes for vegetable dyes, written on the fly-leaf of a George III prayer book, were also hers. This book belonged to my grandmother and she supposed it had been handy when the recipes were given, perhaps by a friend after church. There is a long list of plants and colours: yellow, from dyer's rocket; warm-brown – gorse; purplish – elderberries; carmine – inner bark of birch tree; blue – buttercup root; green – very young heather shoots; magenta – dandelion; pale blue – privet; black – oak; grey – silver birch bark.

'Cut the flowers, leaves, stalks, etc., very small, and put in a tin saucepan close covered with a sufficient quantity of Chamber Lee (urine) to stew for half an hour; strain out the herbs and add a fresh quantity of herbs to make the dye stronger. Then strain again after second boiling and add a lump of alum. In this, dye what you want.'

Another recipe tells to boil the herbs in plain soft water, later adding alum, milk, vinegar, or salt to 'set' the colour. This liquid was kept for six weeks or more before use.

Other dyes I have been told are warm brown from haws; yellow from chamomile; purple from lichen; yellow from southernwood; and from the alder three colours – red from the bark, green from the flowers, and brown from the twigs. A bright green dye, used to colour Easter eggs, was obtained from the pasque-flower.

BIRTH AND BAPTISM

'Hush, my babe, lie still and slumber,
Holy angels guard they bed.'

WATTS

Old countrywomen would say births were most likely to occur when the moon was 'on the change' (just as the new moon came in) than at any other time; they also thought that if a birth occurred when the moon was waxing, the next child would be of the same sex as the last born, but if a waning moon, the opposite sex.

Birthmarks were often blamed on to something which the mother had wished to eat during her pregnancy and had not been able to obtain. But much worse, according to these 'old wives', was for the mother-to-be's path to be crossed by a hare, for this meant the baby would surely be hare-lipped. The only way to prevent this calamity was for the mother's shift to be split from hem to neck — and done at once!

A child born on Christmas Day, or Eve, or on a Sunday, was likely to be good and beautiful, and likely to see spirits; so was a 'chime child' (one born between midnight and 1 a.m. between a Friday and Saturday)[12] and none of them can be overlooked or bewitched. If a child was born in a cawl, he would never be drowned, provided the cawl was preserved. (My grandfather, born in a cawl, lived to ninety-two.) A child should be carried upstairs before being taken downstairs, thus he will 'rise in life'. A first gift to a baby should be a silver coin or an egg.

It was considered unlucky to bring a new cradle into

[12] Miss Ruth Tongue, author and folklorist.

a house before the birth of the baby, while to rock an empty cradle was said to 'rock in' another infant. Should a woman want no more children, she kept the cradle in the house – if it were given away, another birth would follow, however unlikely it might seem at the time. (My grandmother gave hers, with other baby possessions, to her eldest daughter, who was expecting her first child. Grandmother was then forty-eight years old and had had twelve children; four months before her fiftieth birthday, she had her thirteenth.)

It was considered unlucky, too, to say the baby's name on the christening day before it was spoken at the font. If both boys and girls were together at the font, the boys must be baptised first, otherwise they would have no beards when they grew up – unlike the girls who took their place ! It was also unlucky to wipe the baptismal water from the baby's face; it must be allowed to dry naturally.

It was thought to be a bad omen if the baby sneezed ('sneezing its soul out of its body') during the ceremony, and much worse if it did not cry when the water touched it, as crying was considered a sign that the Devil was driven out of the child. It was also unlucky to wash the baby's right hand until after baptism – this ensured his becoming rich. Fingernails were not cut until the child was a year old – until then the mother bit them off; if they were cut, the child would be a thief. And the old adage ran : 'Shorten in May, shorten away.' Water from the font was said to be good for ague, and also for rheumatism.

A child born with big ears was assured of success in life : since the 'little folk' also have big ears, they will take care of it. Some mothers always dressed their babies' feet first, taking care not to put a garment over the child's head for fear of bringing it bad luck. It was also quoted :

'A dimple in his cheek, his living he must seek,
A dimple in his chin, his living will come in.'

If a baby's teeth were quick to appear, old wives would predict another baby in that family quite soon, and quote, 'Soon teeth – soon toes'.

BRIDAL LORE

'I will give you the keys of my heart,
And we will wed 'till death do us part.'

OLD SONG

When we were all children we used to tell our fortune with a piece of ryegrass, chanting, 'Tinker, tailor, soldier, sailor, rich man, poor man, beggar man, thief,' though some of us substituted 'apothecary' for 'beggar man'. Or else we counted the stones left on the plate after eating cherry or plum pie : 'This year, next year, sometime, never.' An old lady who was a native of Hampshire varied this : 'He loves me, he don't, he'll have me, he won't – he would if he could, but he can't'; and yet another chant ran, 'A gift – a friend – a foe – a lover to come – a lover to go.'

As girls grew somewhat older a favourite way of divining the wedding time in the Pewsey Vale was for the couple to go to a stream or pond when the first moon of the year was still waxing, but near to full moon; here they looked at the reflection of the moon in the water through a silk handkerchief – preferably blue in colour –

and as many 'moons' as were thus seen, so many months – or years – away was their wedding day.

When the wedding day was actually fixed there were many superstitions. It was considered very unlucky for engaged couples to hear their own banns read in church; even more so was for the marriage to be cancelled after the third reading, which was said to be 'mocking the church'. Some people thought it unlucky for a girl to marry a man whose surname began with the same letter as her own — and quoted,

> 'Change the name and not the letter,
> change for worse and not for better.'

The time of the wedding was important: hardly any girls would marry during the month of May and this belief has been held for nearly two thousand years. Also it was often said,

> 'If you marry in Lent, you live to repent.'

This was, of course, prohibited in pre-Reformation days, and there is a verse in the Sarum Missal regarding this:

> 'When Avent comes, do thou refraine
> Till Hillary sets ye free again;
> Next Septuagesima saith ye nay,
> But when Low Sunday comes thou may;
> But at Rogation thou must tarry
> Till Trinitie shalt bid ye marry.'

The colour of the wedding dress was all important. An old book says, 'It is not good for a maiden to be married in colours, nor a widow in white, yet let her by all means avoid green or yellow.' Another saying was, 'Yellow is forsaken, green is forsworn.' And every girl seems to know the rhyme about the bride's attire :

> 'Something old and something new,
> Something borrowed and something blue,
> And a sixpence in her shoe.'

The 'something old' seems particularly to appertain to the wedding veil, for it was thought to be very lucky to wear a veil worn by earlier happy brides, as the happiness would be transmitted to the new bride. But she must not see herself in it until the last glance at herself in the mirror just before she left for the church, or the luck would be lost. It was said to be unlucky for the bride and groom to see each other on the wedding day till they met in church. A man going to be married who met a man friend should rub his elbow to ensure good luck.

It is said, 'Happy is the bride the sun shines on,' and this also applies if she should see a rainbow, or meet a sweep or a black cat. It was also considered lucky to marry in a snow storm. When horse-drawn transport was used, it was lucky to use grey horses, and it is still lucky to see one; also, when the bride had been set down at the church door, the coachman was expected to drive on a little way before turning, since to turn immediately was to bring bad luck.

It was thought lucky for the bridesmaids to throw away a pin on the wedding day – but very unlucky to be pricked by one. Bridesmaids also were supposed to have a piece of the wedding cake to put under their pillow that night, to dream of their future husband. This should first have been passed through a wedding ring, some say three times, others think nine.

To drop the wedding ring, particularly in church, fore-told all sorts of ill luck, and the breaking of the ring at any time meant loss of the husband, by death or desertion. Some thought the wedding ring must never be removed, and if it accidentally happened, the husband should put the ring on again; other people said it was all right to re-move the wedding ring after the birth of the first child, and often the bride kept the top tier of her wedding cake to be used at the first child's christening.

A bride must leave for the church and honeymoon by the front door and at her new home she must enter by it, or her life in that house would be unlucky. A farmer and his bride should cross the threshold of their home for the first time side by side – thus they would work well in double harness!

People still seem to throw shoes after the departure of the bridal pair, or tie them on to their conveyance. These must be old shoes, never new ones, to bring luck. Should you want to change your luck, turn your wedding ring round on your finger – this will alter your luck from bad to better. Lastly, this is what an old Wiltshire woman told me, years ago. She said, 'Whoever goes to sleep first on the wedding night will be sure to die first. This is as true as scripture – at least, they say so.'

DEATH AND BURIAL

'My life has been the common lot,
Love, pleasure, sorrow, God knows what;
Now is the time for me to die
And I am sorry, God knows why.
I'll sleep, with all the rest of men,

Perhaps to waken, God knows when,
And in His presence make my bow,
And apologia – God knows how.'

O. E. ELLIS

The 'bodings' of death are numerous. I even knew one
elderly lady[13] who was very anxious about birds looking
in at her window; she declared a robin had tapped on the
window pane just before the death of her late husband.
The owl is another unlucky bird, particularly should it
rest upon a thatched roof. I have myself seen an owl so
perched, and in daylight, once on a thatched roof, and
once on a tiled one. This latter was the rectory at Wootton
Rivers, and the rector, the Reverend R. J. Donne, died
very soon afterwards. The thatched roof was of Oak Farm,
Wilcot, and my aunt who lived there also died shortly
afterwards. In fact, many Wiltshire folk consider owls to
be unlucky to be near a dwelling in any circumstance,
even if only on a brass door-knocker; I once put one on a
back door and the consternation caused was considerable.

Many old county families have some sort of sign which
appears where the death of a member is imminent, but
none of the Wiltshire great houses seem to be so haunted.
The House of Thynne has something of the sort; at Long-
bridge Deverill is a wall, known as the Jew's Wall, and said
to be all that remains of the family house in which Sir
John Thynne lived before he built Longleat. Legend tells
that when this wall falls, then the Marquess of Bath's
family will also fall. It is kept in good repair!

Littlecote House has an ancient elm at the entrance
gates known as Darrell's Tree; it is said to flourish with

[13] Mrs. W. Rutter.

the fortune of the house. The old tree *is* falling into decay, but one or two saplings from the original stock have been allowed to spring up, so it is hoped this will suffice to ensure the continued prosperity of Littlecote.

It forebode death, or very bad luck, if a drill went unsown from one end of a field to the other; this was when seed was sown broadcast. For a dog to howl about a house at night was also thought to predict a death shortly in the house, particularly of the dog's master. Other fatal omens were supposed to be a trio of butterflies flying together, or a candle guttering for no special reason; and ticks in oak beams of old houses (death watch beetles?) warned the inhabitants of some misfortune – often of death.

It used to be thought no one could die comfortably under the cross-beams of a house. And to be lying on a pillow or feather-bed in which were pigeons' feathers, or those of any game bird, was even worse. If a corpse lay unburied over a Sunday, three more deaths in the parish would soon follow, while a death in the parish during Christmastide was thought to be a token of many deaths in the coming year.

In some places salt on a plate was placed on the corpse – said to prevent the body swelling. The front door was left unlocked as long as the corpse remained in the house, or the free passage of the soul would be impeded. Of the funeral itself it was said, 'Blessed is the dead the rain rains upon.' The coffin must always leave the house by the house's front door, which was left to stand open until the mourners returned. If it was closed, a second death would occur in the house very soon after.

Should a coffin be carried along any private path, it was

thought the path was then open to the public. In some parishes people disliked one of their family being the first to be buried in a new churchyard or cemetery, as the first body was said to have to act as guardian of the graveyard. Indeed, it was suggested that some sextons buried the body of a black dog there – on the north side – and this was said to take over the guardian's task.

Finally, a perhaps ironic word about the coffin rings which were sometimes dug up in churchyards when a new grave was being dug : they were often fashioned into rings and worn as a preventative of cramp.

CHRISTMAS FEASTING

'Now all the neighbours' chimneys smoke,
The Christmas logs are burning :
The ovens they with baked meat choke,
And all their spits are turning.'

Great-grandmother made her Christmas puddings in the week following 'Stir-up Sunday', the last Sunday before Advent. (The name was derived from the collect for that day, which began : 'Stir up, we beseech thee, the hearts of thy faithful people.') Everyone in the family was called to stir the mixture, and woe betide anyone who happened to spill any – it was a certain sign they would be prevented in some way from eating any. The pudding had to be stirred with a wooden spoon, in memory of the wooden manger, and, as we stirred, we wished three times for luck (in memory of the Three Wise Men), stirring from east to west, the way the sun travels, because they came from the east. One of the three wishes was supposed to come true within the year, often before the passing of three months.

Mincemeat, stored in a huge yellow and brown stone pot, was also concocted, in readiness for mince pies. In those days minced meat was actually one of the ingredients. My grandmother's[14] recipe says, '1½lb. of beef, coarse, boiled and minced', my grandfather's mother's 'Take a bullock's heart' – while my husband said his mother[15] used chopped lean pig meat. I use none of these, but I do still put in a sprig of rosemary; the old recipe book says, 'When making mincemeat remember to add a sprig of rosemary, for then the sweetmeat be vastly improved and your household shall have luck during the year.'

Mince pies in the old days were often baked in oval, not round, tins, and called manger cakes. I still have such a set of tins which belonged to my great-great-grandmother.[16] Mince pies, too have their own magic : if you eat twelve of them, from twelve separate friends, during the twelve days of Christmas, you are promised a lucky twelve months to follow.

In Wiltshire it seems that goose was the favoured dish for the Christmas dinner. My mother-in-law, who was a great goose-rearer (feeding them on barley meal mixed with skim milk from her butter and cheese making), always cooked at least three geese during a year. The first, a green goose, cooked when the gooseberry was ripe and eaten with gooseberry sauce, was called a gooseberry goose, and eaten unstuffed. The second, a larger bird, eaten for Michaelmas, was stuffed and eaten with apple sauce. But

---

[14] Jane Eleanor Palliser.
[15] Emma Matilda Wiltshire, née Thomas.
[16] Anne Exelby.

the really huge bird was the Christmas goose, stuffed with sage and onion and truffles and served with onion and apple sauces. The fat which drained from this bird was carefully saved, for this was the precious goose grease, that sovereign remedy for stiff backs, bruises, and cow's sore udders!

On Christmas Eve frumenty was always eaten : to make it, kibbled wheat was simmered in milk for about twelve hours (often cooked in a stone pot in the oven), then it was mixed with butter, mixed spice, sugar, raisins, cream, and for the adults, rum. (One farmer I knew described frumenty as 'gruel, with its best clothes on'.) It tastes very like liquid spice loaf, and is very delightful. You can make it with barley instead of wheat – it was called fluffle, and was flavoured with nutmeg only, and laced with brandy.

I well remember sitting on my grandmother's huge steel flat-topped kitchen fender with a bowl of frumenty before going 'up the wooden hill' to await Father Christmas. This was after the excitement of 'Snapdragon'. This always took place in the kitchen round the big scrubbed-top table on Christmas Eve. The largest dish, the 'goose dish' – or the even larger one, made to hold a sucking pig, which had a special trough at one end to catch the gravy – was warmed, placed in the middle of the table, and piled with stoned raisins. With the kitchen in darkness except for the firelight, whisky – or brandy – was poured over the raisins and a lighted match applied. The whole house party, about sixteen strong, and including grandfather, stood around the table and snatched the blazing fruit. What you seized, you could eat! When the dish was empty, saltpetre was strewn on to the remaining whisky, and the faces round the table took on weird hues of violet, green and yellow.

After the children were in bed, the elders tried the Yule bread, in which there were raisins and peel, and which was eaten with cheese and washed down with egg flip. To make this, ale was put to heat on the fire in a copper horn or muller, while three or four eggs were beaten up with four ounces of sugar, a teaspoonful of ginger and nutmeg, and a quarter of good old rum or brandy. When the ale was near to the boil, it was put into one pitcher, and the rum, eggs, etc., into another, and these were turned from one pitcher to the other until all was as smooth as cream. Grandfather called this 'a yard of flannel'.

EGG AND CHICK MAGIC

There was a saying that you should never burn egg shells, or your hens would cease to lay. Many farmers' wives thought it unlucky to bring eggs into the house after sunset; even worse luck would follow if you sold eggs to anyone after that time; and if you bought a setting of eggs, you were careful not carry them over running water, or you would have no chicks in the setting. 'Breast plate' eggs – that is, flat-sided eggs – were thought to be a sign of a death in the family; and 'cocks' eggs' – very small eggs, often containing no yolk – must not be taken into the house or bad luck would follow. It was customary to throw them over the barn (or some building) to avert this. But the first egg laid by a pullet was lucky and was often given as a gift to a man's sweetheart.

Mr. Chanticleer crowing in front of the house door was

thought to be a sign of a coming visitor : if his tail faced the door, this would be a woman, but if the cock faced the door, a man would be expected. The crowing of a cock was also said to scare away fiends. Should a hen copy him and try to crow, this foretold the death of a member of the family; the only way to avert it was to chop off the hen's head. Hence the saw : 'A whistling woman and crowing hen are two of the unluckiest things under the sun.'

There were other bad signs, too. Poultry going to roost at midday could mean the death of the farmer; to save a stock-cockerel from your own breed could bring bad luck with his chicks; and it was also said, 'When the cock crows on going to bed, he wakes in the morning with a wet head.'

To find two yolks in an egg at Easter was lucky. The Easter eggs, I remember, were always coloured by being boiled with various things. Onion-skin in the egg water dyed the eggs yellow; spinach made them green, pasque-flowers a very bright green, and walnut leaves a warm brown. Something was used to make red-coloured eggs, also – perhaps cochineal? We thought them wonderful. We always wore something new for Easter Day, and the meals were traditional : either leg of pork, stuffed with 'robin-in-the-hedge' (ground ivy), or veal, with sorrel sauce (to remind us of the bitter herbs of the Passover). These were often followed by tansy pudding or cake.

SHROVETIDE AND MAY DAY

On Pancake Day at Berwick St. James all the children used to go around the village, beginning at the Hall, and at each big house they would sing a song which ran :

> 'Please, ma'am, I've come a-shroving,
> For a piece of pancake,
> Or a little chuckle cheese,
> Of your own making.
> Is the piece hot?
> Is the piece cold?
> Is the piece in the pot,
> Nine days old?'

They used to be given a penny each, and apples all round. Another rhyme sometimes sung at Winterbourne Stoke was:

'Shrove Tuesday, Ash Wednesday, poor Jack went to plough,
His mother made pancakes, she didn't know how,
She tossed them, she turned them, she made them so black,
She put so much pepper, she poisoned poor Jack.'

Someone who signed herself 'Christian Malford' wrote in 1939 to tell me that when she was a girl fifty years before and living in the village of Winterbourne Gunner, on Shrove Tuesday mornings children would come to their house (sometimes standing 'ankle-deep in snow'), to chant this doggerel:

'Shrovetide is here; we've come a-shroving
For an apple, or an egg, or a little truckle cheese of your own
    making,
Or a bit of pancake (*crescendo* and *ff*).'

She added that her father, who was devoted to children, always aimed to have a supply of coppers ready for the occasion, supplemented with baskets of apples and oranges. On some farms on Pancake Day the first pancake was thrown to the cockerel in the yard; if he ate it all up himself, the crops that year would be scanty, but if he called the hens to share it the crops would be plentiful.

Crowning a May queen seems to have continued right into the twentieth century. When I was a small girl I remember a queen being crowned at Sandridge School, near Melksham. Her crown was made from hawthorn blossoms, and the attendants all wore daisy-chains around neck and wrists. Another hawthorn crown was carried in front of the procession on three long sticks.

Amesbury, at its May Day celebration had the dance of the May queen before the chimney sweep – no one seems to know why.

Durrington kept up Old May Day (13th May). On the previous evening the men of the village went up to the downs and cut a may bush, which they brought back to the Nag's Head Inn, where the maypole was kept. The bush was tied to the top of the maypole, which was then taken to the remains of the old stone cross by the church-yard gate. There it was chained to the stones. On the following evening (Old May Day) a feast was held around it, and the *men* danced around the maypole to the accompaniment of whistle-piper and concertinas.

V

AROUND THE GARDEN

'The kiss of the sun for pardon,
The song of the birds for mirth,
One is nearer to God in a garden
Than anywhere else on earth.'

GARDENS AND ORCHARDS

Nearly all old gardens had one or more apple trees in them; in fact, when a piece of common land was enclosed (that is, when a house with its surrounding garden arose on it) the owner was obliged to plant an apple tree thereon, and thus the lord of the manor, who owned the common land, preserved his rights over the land and was entitled to an annual tithe of fruit. Apple trees were also one of the three things[1] which could only be paid for in living objects, such as young calves or pigs.

Apples were always considered a magic fruit, right from the time of Eve in the Garden of Eden. In our own English legends it was to the Vale of Avalon – the Apple Vale – that King Arthur was taken for the healing of his wounds. Small wonder then the apple was used in divining the identity of the future husband : one had only to peel an apple in one continuous strip and throw it over the left shoulder, and the initial thus formed would be that of the lucky man. Apples, too, had curative properties : as a cure for warts, an apple was cut in half and the warts rubbed by both halves, which were then tied together and buried in the soil. As the apple rotted, so the warts were said to disappear. Poultices made of rotten apples were also used to relieve rheumatism.

Old country folk used to hope to see the sun shine through the bare branches of their apple trees on Christmas morning – some preferred New Year's Day – as they believed this to be an omen for a good crop of apples that year. But apple blossom showing in autumn on a tree bearing its crop of apples was considered most unlucky and predicted a death in the family of the owner.

Another very old belief was that apples were not fit to be eaten until they had been 'christened' by rain on or after St. Swithin's Day.[2] St. Swithin was the Bishop of Winchester (d. A.D. 862) who, as he lay on his deathbed,

---

[1] The others were a swarm of bees, and wooden bowls turned from ivy, holly or hazel wood.
[2] 15th July.

requested his monks to make his grave outside his cathedral, 'where the feet of those going to pray walk over me, and the rain from heaven falls on my burial place'. This order was obeyed, but as the years went by and the fame of the Good Bishop grew the monks decided in 971 that so great and good a man should lie before the high altar in a rich shrine. A day was therefore fixed on which the body of St. Swithin was to be taken from his grave; but when it dawned the rain began to fall torrentially and continued for forty days, until the monks decided not to move the body from its lowly grave. The superstition about rain on St. Swithin's Day is very widely known – there will be rain, 'little or much', on the next forty days. However, old John Green of All Cannings once told me, 'I've a'known it pour wi' rain all day on St. Swithin's and then have a month o' wonnerful vine weather.'

The great St. Dunstan (A.D. 909-98) was another saint of Wessex with a connection with the apple tree. Though he was born and buried in Glastonbury, he was also much concerned with Wiltshire, and the story relating to him which I like best tells of his calling a gathering of the Witan in the town of Calne, when the marriage of the clergy was amongst the matters to be discussed. This was frowned on by the Archbishop, but he seemed to be in the minority until, suddenly, the whole floor collapsed except for the beam which upheld the Saint's chair. This 'miracle' caused the rest of the gathering to agree to Dunstan's ideas. I wonder whether it was 'arranged'?

In his youthful days it was whispered that Dunstan had dabbled in magic, some people even said black magic. In his fields near Glastonbury he grew a good deal of corn, wheat and barley, and he was a great brewer of beer. Wessex folk had always been drinkers of cider, and this taste lessened the sale of the beer; so, it was said, Dunstan made a pact with the Devil that the Devil would bring frost to the apple blossoms on Dunstan's birthday – 19th May – and lessen the apple crop.[3]

According to tradition, when Satan was thrown out of Heaven, he fell to earth right into the middle of a blackberry clump; whereupon he cursed the plant. We were always told we must never pick blackberries after 28th October, Saint Simon and Saint Jude's Day, for after that day the berries belonged to the Devil and he spat upon them, or urinated on them, or scorched them with his breath, or threw his club over the bush – take your pick!

The elder tree had dozens of superstitions attached to it. To burn elder wood was most unlucky – you would bring the Devil into the house. If a child was laid in an elderwood cradle it would pine away, or be pinched black and blue by the fairies. If a child was whipped with an elder stick its growth would be stunted. The traditional wood for cradles was birch, which was said to drive away evil spirits.

Many of the funerary flint arrowheads found in old barrows are shaped like an elder leaf. Is that why some cattle when ill were thought to have been hit by these flint arrows – 'elf-shot'?

Blackthorn trees were trees of black magic; the thorns

[3] Yet another tale tells that Dunstan, who was a skilled smith – chiefly of gold and silver – was busy at his forge one day when he was visited by a beautiful woman. But the Saint noticed she had cloven feet beneath her long robes, and seized the Devil by the nose with his blacksmith's pinchers.

from them were used to stick into the wax images that witches made to resemble their enemies and the wood of the blackthorn was often used as a witch's walking stick.

It used to be said a whitethorn (hawthorn) growing near a blackthorn would destroy the blackthorn; and I have also heard it said that if a hawthorn growing in a hedge dies and is replaced by a young hawthorn, the young tree never thrives – indeed, it generally dies. I wonder if this theory bears upon the hedge at the Bell, Malmesbury, which is said always to die, however often replanted, where the 'grey lady' passes through?[4]

It seems a moot point as to whether blackthorn or whitethorn or elder was used for the log, traditionally placed by a witch in her bed, crowned by her nightcap, when she was away visiting her covens. Her password regarding this to a sister-witch was said to be 'I slept like a log last night'.

As for the occasional large tree in a hedge, it was said, 'Set them at All Hallows (1st November) and command them to prosper, but set them at Candlemas (2nd February) and entreat them to grow.' A waxing moon was also essential and a Tuesday or a Friday planting made it more likely the tree would prosper.

The ash tree had associations of good fortune. A traditional good luck wish ran, 'May your footfall be by the root of an ash'; and Jesus was said to have had his first bath before a fire of ashlogs.

In Wiltshire runner beans were sown on Calne Fair Day (6th June).[5] In leap years it was said beans would grow

[4] See my *Ghosts and Legends of the Wiltshire Countryside*, p. 107.
[5] Mr. H. Gay, sen.

wrong side up. A white plant in a row of beans was thought a death omen for some relation of the family, while should anyone fall asleep in a bean field (and the strong scent of the flowers and the drone of the many honey bees were inclined to make anyone drowsy) he would thereafter have nightmares and might even go mad.

The bean was also a wart curative; one rubbed the wart with the woolly lining inside the beanpod.[6] The pod is, of course, buried and allowed to rot. Old gardeners would say :

'Sow peas and beans (broad) on David and Chad,
Whether the weather is good or bad.'

(St. David's Day falls on 1st March, and St. Chad's follows on 2nd. March) Another version ran :

'When parson begins the Bible, 'tis time to till the beans.'

This is on Septuagesima Sunday; and 'Peas and beans should lie so thin that a ewe and her lamb may lie within.'

Herbs generally had some mystic power to expound something. For instance, rosemary grows best 'where the missus is the master'; and, similarly, sage tells that the wife 'wears the breeches'. 'Sage set in May, will never decay';[7] and it also 'likes to grow' with marjoram. And if you plant parsley on Good Friday, you will never be short of it.

Madonna lilies were often seen in old gardens, maybe because these flowers were supposed to keep away ghosts. If a bay tree died in a garden it used to be a warning of a

[6] Mrs. Harry Gay, jun. I have only heard of this being used in Wiltshire.
[7] John Cook, All Cannings.

death – some people say a death in the royal family – and bay leaves were thrown on to the fire before a journey or some new project, to see if they would crackle – which meant good luck to plans made. If no crackle, no luck.

It was unlucky to burn holly branches while they were green, but lucky to have a holly tree in the garden. It guarded the house against thunder and lightning and was a strong protection against witches and the Evil Eye. Incidentally, should you be troubled by a witch, you only had to steal a piece of the thatch of her house (while she was in there), take it home to sprinkle it with salt and water and set fire to it. The ash so obtained had to be buried at the change of the moon – then all the witch's power against you would be lost.

It was considered that ivy growing on a house protected those within from all evil, but should the ivy suddenly wither, misfortune of some sort would happen.

The marigold had several uses : it was used to flavour soups and cakes, and to make butter and cheese a brighter yellow colour; it was said to cure wasp or bee stings; and it was even sometimes used to dye the hair. But the use I like the most I found written in an old notebook : 'On St. Luke's Day (18th October) take marigold flowers, a sprig of marjoram, and of thyme, and a little wormwood, dry them before a fire, then rub them to powder, and sift through a fine piece of lawn. Simmer this with a small quantity of virgin honey in white vinegar; with this anoint your stomach, breast and lips, lying down, and repeat these words thrice :

> 'St. Luke, St. Luke, be kind to me,
> In dreams let me my true love see.'

This said, hasten to sleep, and in the soft slumber of your night's repose, the very man whom you shall marry shall appear before you.'

The pretty nigella was a favourite flower of my sister-in-law,[8] but she called it 'devil-in-a-bush' while I, copying my grandmother, called it 'love-in-a-mist'. This is said to be St. Catherine's own flower; the seed is to be sown on 30th April, the day of St. Catherine of Sienna, then the flowers should be blooming on the day sacred to St. Catherine of Genoa, 14th September. The great St. Catherine, martyr of Alexandria, had her special day on 25th November, when Catherine pears are fit for eating – as they were said to ripen about Martinmas (11th November). Sir John Suckling, in his 'Ballad upon a Wedding' wrote :

> 'Her cheeks so faire a white was on
> No daisy makes comparison,
> Who sees them is undone;
> For streaks of red were mingled there
> Such as are on a Catherine pear,
> The side that's next the sun.'[9]

All old gardens had some rose bushes – a pink moss-rose, and a Maiden's Blush the old red cabbage rose, with perhaps the Gloire de Dijon's yellow flowers on the garden wall. But in my grandmother's day – and her grandmother's day also – roses were used in cookery, medicinal concoctions, and beauty aids. Rose petal jam was made from three or four cupfuls of red or pink petals, added to an equal number of cupfuls of white sugar, which, with a

[8] Miss Elizabeth Wiltshire.
[9] cf. 'Catherine-pear coloured beads' (*Westward Ho* !).

tablespoonful of lemon juice and a cupful of rose-water, had been allowed to dissolve; you then put it in 'the rays of the mid-day sun' to amalgamate, and then cooked over a very low heat, stirring all the time (for it burns very easily) for half an hour. When the petals were transparent or melted, it stood to cool and was then put into small pots.

Nor was this the only way rose petals were used. 'Confection of Roses' was said to be good for delicate chests : it was made by beating up fresh rose petals with white sugar. Rose toffee was made from red rose petals; and an infusion of rose petals, acidulated with sulphuric acid and slightly sweetened, was found 'a pleasant vehicle for other medicine'. Candied petals (not only of roses but of many flowers) were used as sweetmeats, being variously reputed to cure colds, remedy bad temper, heal wounds, or induce sleep.[10] Candied myrtle blossoms were supposed to beautify the complexion.

In our village, in the 1890s, old men of the district would appear at the back door, particularly after a spell of wet weather, with the request, 'Can we look for wall fruit?' This was their local name for snails, which they removed from crannies in the walls and other likely places; these they then boiled over the fire at the blacksmith's forge and later sold at the inn for so many a penny.[11] But the wise woman of the village considered snails as a cure for consumption and other diseases of the chest, and they were very favoured by workers in snuff and tobacco factories. Violet jam, which has been made since the time of Charles II, was also said to be a cure for consumption.

[10] Lettuce was another antidote for insomnia.
[11] H. J. Wiltshire.

I was once given an old recipe[12] said to be called mock asses' milk, for which you layer one pound of snails in salt and water for two days, after which they were cleaned and washed; to them was added a quarter of a pound of barley and threepennyworth of eryngo-root; boil all together until they become a jelly and let them be strained off; half a pint was taken at night and again in the morning by a grown person, and a quarter pint for a child. This was considered an excellent remedy for consumption or any weakness. It was also whispered that some unscrupulous farmers used snails, bruised in milk and boiled, to add to cream. In fact, one seller of milk in Swindon district years ago is reported to have stated they were the most successful imitation for cream that he knew.

Carnations were said to have first been grown in English gardens to spice the wine and ale when Indian cloves were too expensive. In more recent years they became used as cures.

An old Wiltshire woman[13] once told me her husband had always brought her a bunch of the small wild pansies, often called 'love in idleness', from amongst the ripening corn. But he called them 'love-a-li-dells'. Certainly 'love in idleness' was Shakespeare's name for this flower, in *A Midsummer Night's Dream* :

'Yet marked I where the bolt of Cupid fell :
It fell upon a little western flower
Before milk-white; now purple with love's wound,
And maidens call it Love in Idleness.'

Three names for the pansy are heart's ease, three faces

12 Mrs. James.
13 Mrs. Harriet Draper.

under one hood (this from its three colours), and herb trinity. But other names were much more fanciful: Johnny-jump-up, call-me-to-you, look up and kiss me, kiss me at the garden gate, kiss me ere I rise, or – strangest of all – meet her i' the entry, and kisses her i' the butter.

Nasturtiums were used by our grandmothers to make a pickle which they used in place of caper sauce : the seeds were gathered on a dry hot day and put into glass bottles, with vinegar, salt, and pepper – one ounce of salt and six peppercorns to each pint of vinegar – and the corks were rosened. It was kept for ten or twelve months before use. The young leaves and flowers of the nasturtiums, which are of a slightly hot nature, were also used in salads. Old country people would always leave a little of the crop behind in a field or garden; this they said would ensure a good crop the next year.

BEES IN YOUR BONNET

'Busy bees of Paradise,
Do the work of Jesus Christ,
Do the work which no man can.
God made man, and man made money,
God made the bees and bees made honey,
God made the big man to plough, reap and sow,
God made the little man to shoo off the crow.'

TRADITIONAL ENGLISH SONG

Over 1,000 years ago bees were considered sufficiently important for King Howel the Good of Wales to draw up a number of laws concerning them. A hive of bees he valued at twenty-four pence, and every swarm before August was worth as much. During August the price fell, but no swarm was worth more than four pence until it had settled for three days – 'A day to find a place, a day to remove, a day to rest, and at all time in serene weather.'

Old churchmen decreed that the candles used for the mass must be made of beeswax and at the service used the words, 'This solemn offering of wax candles, the work of the bees'. Unluckily, witches also valued this, and often stole the mass candles to use in their practices.

Legend has it that the bees in the Garden of Eden were white, but turned brown after the Fall; also that in their hives at midnight on Christmas Eve the bees sing the 100th Psalm, 'O be joyful in the Lord, all ye lands'. We are told they object strongly to blasphemy and swearing (they sting to punish it) and to inchastity. The stings, on the other hand, are also said to avert rheumatism.

My grandmother used to tell me when I was a child that on 12th March St. Gregory opens the flowers for the bees, and on 21st March St. Benedict calls the bees forth for their year's garnering. She also said the bees would not accept the good Saint's invitation unless the owners had remembered to rouse them on Christmas morning with a gentle knock and the message, 'Christ is born'.

Bees flying round a sleeping child are said to bring luck to it. They are also weather 'boders', or prophets :

> 'If bees stay at home, rain will soon come,
> If they fly away, fine will be the day.'

Wiltshire people used to say if a bumble bee came into the house, some person would also come there to 'breed a row'.[14] Many people believed no luck would follow if you

[14] Miss E. House, Wilcot.

paid money for a swarm of bees; some living thing must be given in exchange, such as a small pig, or a sack of corn, which were considered the worth of a May swarm.

> 'A swarm of bees in May is worth a load of hay,
> A swarm of bees in June is worth a silver spoon,
> A swarm of bees in July is not worth a fly.'

A Wiltshire man, Mr. Fred King, of Stanton, once told me that if a swarm settles on your land you can take it, but you must take your door key and knock with it three times on the box you have put them in (having first rinsed it out with sugar water) and say, 'Bees! Bees! Bees! You now belongs to ——. Work for him faithfully, and he will look after you and feed you in winter.'

It is said[15] bees like to be told of all their owner's doings and troubles; if a bee-master dies the new owner must go round the hives and bow to each, and tap the hives with the house key and say, 'Your master is dead; you must now work for –' (naming himself). If this is not done the bees either swarm and fly away, or die of a mysterious illness. Some people even used to tie a piece of crepe to each hive to put the bees in mourning for the bee-master. Bees also like to be told if a relation dies, but no name must be spoken : 'Your master's brother from –' took the place of the name. They were told, too, of rejoicing and a piece of wedding cake was left by the hive for them to share in the wedding breakfast.

If bees swarmed high in the trees, country folk said grain prices would be high that year, and if low, prices would fall. If a swarm pitched on to a dead branch or tree,

[15] John Cook, born 1860 in my cottage, Church Hatch, All Cannings.

it was said to foretell a death in the bee-master's family. Little honey being produced was an omen of war, and bees 'nesting' on a house roof was a sign that the daughters of the house would not marry.

Bees sometimes make their home in very odd places. When my husband was a lad, bees were between the floor of his bedroom and the ceiling of a dairy below, in Cliff Farm, All Cannings. They were eventually 'taken' by a Mr. Chitty of Pewsey, a great bee-keeper, who took over forty pounds of honey from this home-made hive. He used the beeswax from it to polish the reredos in Pewsey Church, carved by the rector, Canon Bouverie. My grandmother's home-made furniture polish was made from '3 oz, of beeswax, 1 oz. of white wax, 1 oz. of yellow soap, grated and put into a clean jar, and covered with a pint of hot soft water'. This was placed in the oven, and stirred occasionally. Then a pint of turpentine was mixed in well with the other ingredients, after which the wax was kept in a corked bottle and was ready for use after two days.

LADY MOON

'Thy horns point east –
Shine, be increased !
Thy horns point west –
Wane, be at rest.'

CHRISTINA ROSSETTI

The waxing and waning of the moon was carefully noted by all old gardeners. Seeds of above-ground plants were always sown at the new moon, which as it waxed drew up the plant. 'Watery' plants, such as marrows or cucumbers, were said to flourish best if planted at full moon. 'Underground' plants (potatoes, carrots, etc.) were set when the moon was dark, as the moon would keep them safely in the dark. And timber cut at the dead of the moon was said to dry much more quickly than if cut when the moon was waxing.

A man always 'turns his silver' in his pocket for luck on first seeing a new moon (silver being the metal sacred to the moon-goddess), and maybe also spits on a coin for luck. A woman curtsies – some say three times – and turns the way the moon goes round between each 'bob'. Both wish as they thus salute the 'Shepherdess of Stars'. Some old ladies turned their aprons as they wished. It was dreadfully unlucky to see the new moon for the first time through trees or through glass, the latter idea, I imagine, being much later than the first.

The moon also foretells the coming weather: a ring round the moon predicts wet weather – the nearer the ring the further off the rain. 'A moon on its back catches wet in its lap' – rough, wet and stormy weather; but if a moon should change at 'no hours' (between midnight and 1 a.m.) it is said to be a certain sign of very bad weather. This is often called an 'underground moon' as it changes when the sun is below the earth.

The old Druidical calendar was ruled by the change of the moon and had a month of twenty-eight days with thirteen months in a year. This gave 364 days, and thus gave rise to the often quoted 'a year and a day' in old stories (such as *Sir Gawain and the Green Knight*).

The moon was said to influence bloodflow as well as tides, and blood pressure is thought to increase with it. In his *Natural History,* Pliny gives a long list of the powers –

for good or bad – a menstruating woman possesses. Her touch, he said, could blast vines, ivy and rue, fade purple cloth, blacken linen in the wash tub, tarnish copper, make bees desert their hives, and cause abortion in mares. But she could also rid a field of pests by walking around it naked before sunrise, and cure boils, erysipelas, hydrophobia, and barrenness.

It is strange that the same idea was believed in Wiltshire. I was told in about 1940 (when pigs were often killed in farm houses) that should such a woman handle any of the pig meat or bacon, it would certainly 'go off'. And I have recently heard from Market Lavington that the same belief is held there about jam-making – which either becomes mouldy, or 'goes sugary' if made by such a woman.

It was also said if a pig was killed when the moon was waning, all the fat would run out of the bacon when it was cooked. This bacon would shrink when cooking, while bacon killed at the full of the moon would swell.

Monday – the moon's day – was thought to be the best day to 'set' a hen – you could be sure of a good hatch. You always put an odd number of eggs under the hen, usually thirteen (if you put an even number all the chicks would be cockerels). A cross or dot was marked on the egg shell, said to be a guide that the hen 'turned' her eggs daily, but also to keep the Devil at bay.

Linen was spread out on a grass patch overnight, in the moonlight, and this removed any stains. But nothing was thought to be worse than to allow moonlight to fall upon someone asleep; they would grow 'pasty-looking' and thin, and their eyes become weak. It was also most unlucky to point at the moon – 'If you do so nine times you don't go to Heaven when you die.' Country women used to cut the ends of their hair just before a new moon, to encourage the hair to grow long; and it was said that storage apples must always be picked when the moon was waning – any bruises on these would dry out. If picked when waxing, the bruises would rot and spread.

My aunt's old gardener used to say he set his onion seed on the fourth new moon of the year; and another of his quaint beliefs was that potato seed should never be fetched 'against the sun'. You could buy seed from any place north of you, but never, never, from the south (can this explain a preference for Scotch seed potatoes?).

The moon was also thought to have an effect on wine making. Of wheat wine – which can be as strong as whisky if kept long enough – I was told, 'Be sure to bottle it at full moon and with a north wind blowing if possible.'

Another old proverb ran : 'Light Christmas (full moon), light wheatsheaf; dark Christmas (dead of moon), heavy wheatsheaf.' We were also told when sowing the wheat the farmer must 'Sow one for the mouse, one for the crow, one to rot, and one to grow'. In the days before the present use of dressed seed wheat, a farmer would sprinkle his seed corn with a concoction made by pouring boiling water upon 'blue vitrol' (sulphate of copper).[16] The fumes arising from the preparation were said to be dangerous to inhale, and one was always told to turn one's head away while mixing. In his boyhood my husband used to be sent to hold a lantern in the barn while his father dressed his wheat seed, and for years he imagined this ceremony must be

[16] Copper is one of the metals alchemists ascribed to the moon.

undertaken in the dark, and after the farm workers were gone home.

Finally, never start a venture or a journey when the moon is on the wane.

VI

TOWN AND VILLAGE TALES

Many towns and villages seem to have some old tale –
often somewhat uncomplimentary – handed down from
one generation to another, but sadly they tend now to
become forgotten.

One which has become attached to Wiltshiremen in
general came from the two Cannings villages – Bishops
and All (from the Anglo-Saxon *aeld* – old) Cannings, and
tells why they are generally called 'Wiltshire Moonrakers'.

The tale runs that a party of smugglers had hidden some
brandy kegs in a pond and a group of them were, at dead
of night, fishing these out with the aid of wooden hayrakes,
when they were seen by an exciseman who was riding by.

In reply to his questions, he was told they were raking the water to obtain that fine cheese – pointing to the reflection of the full moon on the surface of the pond. The exciseman rode away laughing, convinced that Wiltshiremen were even stupider than he had thought.

Which pond it was is in dispute. Bishops Cannings villagers used to say they raked the cheese in the Crammer, the large pond by the side of St. James's Church, Devizes, which then was in their parish. But All Cannings folk declare it was from the large pond once by their churchyard, now filled in; but I was told at Beckhampton recently[1] it was the pond by the roadside, outside Cliff Farm, All Cannings, and once on the Green. This pond is also now only a memory.

The church of St. Mary, Bishops Cannings, has a strange small spire built by the side of the large one, and legend tells that once the village folk manured the small spire to help it to grow. And once the greater proportion of the population of Bishops Cannings walked in a body to Devizes Market Place to see a comet, which they heard could be seen from that spot. However, John Aubrey said Bishops Cannings could match all England for music, football and ringing.

Chippenham shares its story with a village nearby, for it was in Langley Burrell that Maud Heath is supposed to have been born. She was a market woman who left money and land to provide a causeway, some four and a half miles long, which begins on Wick Hill and passes through Bremhill Wick, East Tytherton, Kellaways, Langley Burrell, to

[1] By member of Over Sixties Club, Mrs. Munday, née Grant, May 1974.

the outskirts of Chippenham, and thus allowed walkers to pass dry shod over the water meadows of the Avon valley. No doubt she may have gone that way herself in flood times. A monument, set up in 1698, has the inscription, 'To the memory of the worthy Maud Heath, widow. Who in the year of grace, 1474, for the good of travellers, did in charity bestow in land and houses about eight pounds a year for ever, to be laid out in a highway and causey leading from Wick Hill to Chippenham Cliff. This pillar was set up by the feoffees, 1698.' On a tall pillar at the top of Wick Hill, Bremhill, sits a figure of Maud Heath in her old-time attire, carrying a large basket and walking stick.

It is said Langley Burrell's church bells ring, 'My cow's tail's long. My cow's tail's long.'[2]

A lady who once lived at Great Wishford has a very strange story : she was Dame Edith Bonham, whose first children happened to be twins. Why this displeased her husband, Sir Thomas, seems untold, but he departed on a crusade, and was away for seven years. A year after his return his wife had seven children at a birth – the same number as the years of his absence; and these children were all carried to be baptised in Great Wishford church, in a sieve. This sieve was reputed to have hung over the parents' tomb for many years.

Another tale attached to a tomb belongs to Broad Hinton, and is equally strange. This is the tomb of Sir Thomas Wroughton and his wife and family : Sir Thomas, a proud bearded man in armour, and his wife in a Tudor bonnet, holding a Bible, are accompanied by eight child-

[2] John Cole, Kington St. Michael.

ren, four sons and four daughters. Only the mother has hands. The story runs that Sir Thomas's wife was inclined to the Protestant faith, and once her husband found her reading a copy of the Bible in English. Much enraged, he threw the book into the fire, and in so doing he badly burnt his hands. All his children were born without them.

Sherston has a very different hero, who, according to tradition, was named John Rattlebone and fought valorously in the Battle of Sherston between Canute and Edmund Ironside in 1016. A jingle tells :

> 'Fight well, Rattlebone
> Thou shalt have Sherstone.'
> 'What shall I with Sherstone do
> Save with all that belongs thereto?'
> 'Thou shalt have Wych and Wellesley,
> Easton Town and Pinkeney.'

It is said Rattlebone was dreadfully injured in the fight, held a tile to his side, and still fought on. He is thus depicted on the village inn sign. A figure on the east side of the outside of the porch of the church is also said to represent the village hero – the porch dates from the fifteenth century – but this may equally be the figure of an archbishop holding the Gospels.

Devizes' story is not just a legend – it is written, for all to read, on a cross in Devizes Market Place, presented to the town by Lord Sidmouth in 1814 :

'On Thursday, the 25th of January, 1753, Ruth Pierce, of Potterne, in this County, agreed with three other women to buy a sack of wheat in the Market, each paying her due proportion towards the same. One of these women, in collecting the several quotas of money, discovered a deficiency, and demanded of Ruth Pierce the sum which was wanted to make good the amount. Ruth Pierce protested she had paid her share and said "She wished she might drop down dead if she had not." She rashly repeated this awful wish, when, to the consternation and terror of the surrounding multitude, she instantly fell down and expired, having the money concealed in her hand.'

It is said the sack of corn cost 17/- (4/3 to each woman) and when the farmer who sold the corn counted his money he found it threepence short. His name was Nathaniel Alexander.

The tiny village of Seagry, which is about five miles from Chippenham, is somewhat unusual. As there has never been any lord of the manor there is free fishing in the Avon; also, the waste land by the roadside belongs to no one and consequently many houses were built there, which belong to the builders. There is at Seagry a curious tenure called 'key hold'. Whoever has the key of any of these houses built on the Waste is the owner of the house. The Seagry folk thought they were exempt from the operation of the laws of England, and were governed by their own laws and customs. They also have a curious superstition – that if a corpse lies unburied in the place on Twelfth Night there will be twelve deaths in the parish within the year. An old woman related that a young girl came to her cottage and said, 'So and so is lying dead, and this is Twelfth Night; there are sure to be twelve deaths in the parish within the year.' Twelve people did die that year, and the girl was one of the first. The average number of deaths each year was about two.

James Long, who died on 21st October 1768 at the age of seventy-four was buried at Urchfont. His monument (surmounted by a demi-lion, the Long crest) records he was instrumental in procuring the straightening of the main road between Tinkfield and Lydeway : the benefit of this to the public was thought to justify the erection of a monument. Until this new road was made, the highwayman Boulter would often hide in a droveway just above here and pounce on travellers and rob them.

Another headquarters of Tom Boulter, who was born at Poulshot Mill, was an old Pilgrim's Chapel, built in the fifteenth century at Chapel Plaister, near Box. At the east end is a reredos of three canopied arches, the centre one with a semi-circular front, and on the outside is a hole, which perhaps held a lantern to guide pilgrims at night.

Up to 1890 a horn supper was apparently held on the night before Weyhill Fair, at which a metal cup, fixed between a pair of ram's horns, was used.

The Congregational Chapel at Horningsham, near Warminster, was founded in 1566, and claims to be the oldest dissenting place of worship in England.

At the Meeting House at Kington St. Michael (John Aubrey's birthplace – and that of my husband's father) a ranting preacher once said, 'The Methodists bring the lost sheep down off the mountains, the Baptists wash them, and the Church of England shears them.' At Kington St. Michael, too, there is a tradition that during the Great Plague the village streets were green with grass because so few people passed along them.

Charlton, near Malmesbury, is reported to be the birthplace of Moll Davis. She was the daughter of one of the villagers, became an actress, and later one of the favourites of King Charles II.

I first heard of Aldbourne dabchicks when I was a very small girl. An old man named Thomas Hawkins had a smallholding just below my aunt's farm – near Pewsey – and he told me he was an 'Arbourne dabchick'. This sobriquet belongs only to true-born Aldbourne people, and the story he told about it runs thus: 'Long ago a strange bird was seen swimming on the village pond and nobody was sure what kind of bird it was. Somebody suggested that the oldest inhabitant be asked; so, as he could not walk, he was wheeled in a wheelbarrow. They took him three times round the pond and he then pronounced the bird to be a dabchick. From this, the 'Arbourne' native took his nickname – though it was not safe to mention this, particularly during Feast Week, for the scoffer was like to find himself in the pond. Ramsbury folk were great offenders in this respect, and they were said to have on occasion tied a dead dabchick to the back of Aldbourne's carrier's cart.

There is in Aldbourne's church belfry a small Corr bell which has a little water bird engraved inside it. Since the last Corr bell was cast in 1757, it would seem the dabchick has been the symbol of 'Arbourne' village for over 200 years.

Pewsey Feast (or 'Veast') is known all over Wiltshire, and it is believed to date from the time of Alfred the Great, whose statue stands in Pewsey Market Place. It is said Alfred left his Queen in Pewsey when he went to meet the Danes, and promised the people there that if she was safe when he returned they should be granted a yearly feast at

Holy Cross Day – for ever. She was safe when the victorious Alfred returned, so Pewsey had its feast. Whether this story is true or not, there is evidence that Alfred held a council at Swanborough Trump. A trump is a little hillock or barrow mound. About halfway between Pewsey and Woodborough is such a barrow with three tall ashes growing on it. It is in the corner of a field adjoining Frith Wood and is called 'Swanborough Trump' and the trees 'Swanborough Ashes'. In monastic records of the tenth century, it is named 'Swanabeorgh' which means 'barrow of the swains or peasants'. There is no village of Swanborough in Pewsey Vale, but in Saxon times the part of the Vale round the trump was the Swanborough Hundred – the Saxon 'hundreds' being originally divisions of land, each the area in which a hundred invaders had set up their households during the conquest of Britain. In each there was a recognised place at which the 'hundred moot', or council of the district, assembled when called together. For Swanborough Hundred the meeting place was this mound. Alfred the Great wrote in his famous will : 'But it came to pass that we were all harassed with the heathen invasion, then we discussed our children's future – how they would need some maintenance, whatever might happen to us through these disasters. When we were assembled at Swanborough, we agreed, with the cognizance of the West Saxon Council, that whichever of us survived, the other was to give to the other's children the land which we had ourselves acquired, and the lands which King Ethelwulf gave us . . .'

There is evidence, too, that the spot was still used as a hundred meeting place in the eighteenth century. A docu-

ment published in *Notes and Queries,* vol. 2, 1896–98 re-
fers to a court leet in 1764 'to be holden at Swanborough
Ash . . . in and for the said Hundred on Monday the 15th
Day of this instant October'.

Malmesbury was said to have been founded by the
legendary British King Malmud in the fourth century
B.C. (His sons Belinus and Brennus crossed the Alps before Hannibal; Brennus is said to have led the Gauls who
burnt Rome). The Code Malmud (said to have been
brought to England about the time of Abraham) was
written in 'triads', to be more easily memorised. Here are
some of them :

'There are three things that are private and sacred
property to every man, Briton or foreigner – his wife, his
children, his domestic chattels. There are three civil birth-
rights of every Briton – the right to go where he pleases,
the right wherever he is to protection from his land and
sovereign, the right of equal privileges and equal restric-
tions. There are three sons of captives who free themselves
– a bard, a scholar and a mechanic. There are three per-
sons who have a right to public maintenance, the old, the
babe, the foreigner who cannot speak the British tongue.'

In 640, Madulf, an Irish missionary, founded a school
in Malmesbury, to which Ina, King of Wessex, sent his
nephew, Aldhelm, as a pupil. This was St. Aldhelm,
British Bishop of Sherborne, who died in A.D. 700.

The village of Odstock, not far from Salisbury, has the
strange distinction of a curse on the key of the church
door.[3] The story begins sadly, for in the year 1800 a
gipsy who lived in Odstock, named Joshua Scamp, had

[3] This story was told to my uncle by Canon Bouverie, about 1904.

been hanged for the supposed stealing of a horse. It was discovered later he was innocent of the crime, which had been committed by his daughter's husband, who (purposefully, it seems) had left Scamp's coat in the stable from which the horse was taken. To protect his daughter and her unborn child, Scamp refused to plead; he was hanged in Fisherton Jail in 1801 and buried in Odstock churchyard.

The gipsies used to visit his grave on the anniversary of his death, and gradually this pilgrimage deteriorated into unruly gatherings which upset the village.

The rector of Odstock and his churchwardens resolved these gatherings must cease, so they enrolled special constables to preserve order when the anniversary was due. The gipsies retaliated by smashing everything in the church and churchyard they could lay hands upon – cutting the bell-ropes, and pulling up every tree in the churchyard. After visits to the inn, the gipsy queen (who was said to be the mother of the horse thief) came back into the churchyard towards the evening, stood on the wall and surveyed those present. She spoke first to the rector, and declared he would not be preaching there at that time next year. Then she turned to the churchwarden, a farmer named Hodding, and promised him two years of bad luck – 'For two years bad luck shall tread on thy heels.' Next she told the sexton he would be in his grave by next year, and then she cursed two half-gipsies, named Bob and Jack Bachelor, who had become special constables, telling them they would 'die together, sudden and quick'. She ended by saying, 'I put a curse on this church door! From this time whoever shall lock 'un shall die within a year.' (It was said she had been pushed out of the church earlier in the day, and the door had been locked on her.) And all these curses came true.

The rector had a stroke, which affected his speech, so he never again preached a sermon. Farmer Hodding's cows went down with anthrax, and his crops failed. His wife had stillborn infants and the couple left the district. The sexton, who was also a village roadman, was found dead by his barrow one day, apparently from heart failure. The two Bachelor brothers disappeared during the next barley harvest and were never seen again. Many years later two tall skeletons were found in a shallow grave on Odstock down – many thought they were the Bachelors. Maybe the gipsies took steps to see that this part of the curse came true.

As to the church door, it has been locked twice since the curse was put on it, once deliberately and once inadvertently – but both of those who locked the door died within a year. So, some years ago the then rector of Odstock threw the church door key into the river, which he considered the safest place for it.

MURDERS

Many years ago an old farmer was murdered at his home, Little Cuckoo Farm (now part of Church Farm), Urchfont. He had been to market and sold some farm produce very well, and this was noticed by a man, who went to his farm after dark. On being asked inside, he killed the old man, stole the gold and, shutting his dog in the house with his dead master, hurriedly left the village for Tilshead. Soon afterwards a friend of the old farmer came to see him and discovered the murder, and let the dog out. The dog immediately made its way to Tilshead and there the murderer was found drunk, and spending the stolen gold. He was later hanged from a gallows in a field by the farm, since when it has been called 'Gallows Field'.[4]

Thomas Burry had been the landlord of a little thatched inn lying in a lonely spot called Lydeway on the Devizes to Andover road, The Shepherd and Dog. This inn had a bad reputation in the district : it was rumoured several pedlars – or other wealthy-looking travellers – entered the inn and were never heard of again.

There was one tale that a Mr. Withers was drinking in The Shepherd and Dog one evening when he overheard whispers that a Scottish pedlar had come to the inn and was staying the night; and someone, it seemed, was proposing to murder him. Mr. Withers left the inn and ran all the way to the village of Urchfont, where he related what was going on; several of the villagers accompanied him back to the inn, where they managed to rescue the victim through a window.

There was a trap door in a private room where mine host used to invite his victim for a drink; while he was drinking, the bolt was drawn, and the unfortunate man found himself in a cellar, where he was murdered and robbed. The body was then buried in a field behind the inn. Here more than a dozen bodies were dug up from shallow graves and long after Thomas Burry's death a young man unearthed another skeleton which was found to have the skull bashed in. At the inquest many old people who remembered Burry were called to give evidence; one of

[4] Mrs. F. Self.

them, an old inhabitant of Urchfont named Sutton, who was eighty-eight years old, remembered Mr. Withers's story. Other witnesses said the cry of 'Murder' had often been heard in the locality of The Shepherd and Dog at night. Still others related the tradition that Stert church bells refused to sound at Thomas Burry's funeral in 1842. This was at the little church of St. James, rebuilt in 1846. The chalice and cover from the original church date from 1577.

Of course, the inn lost its licence – no trace of the building now remains.

Another strange story involving a murder at Pewsey was told by Canon Bouverie.

In July 1798 a Mr. Taylor Dyke, of Manningford Abbas, had received a large sum of money for some of his farm produce and went to the Phoenix Inn to celebrate. The Phoenix at that time stood on the other side of the road from the present inn, and had yews cut into fantastic figures opposite to it.

Mr. Dyke boasted of the sum of gold he was carrying, and was overheard by other drinkers in the inn. When he left to go to his home by way of the field path over the Cow Ground, he was followed by a man named Amor, who robbed and murdered Mr. Dyke, even taking his watch.

On the next Sunday the rector of Pewsey, the Rev. Joseph Townsend, had the corpse of Mr. Dyke brought into the church (everyone at that time attended church), and as the people went out, they had to lay their hand upon the face of the dead man and declare they were not guilty. When it came to Amor's turn he shrank back, and was later charged with the crime. Mr. Dyke's watch was found in a pond which then was at the rectory gate, after it had been dragged for a week. Amor was hanged on 4th March 1799, by the side of the sheep walk going up to the down. He lived in Quality Court, Pewsey, and it used to be said there were stains on the floor which no amount of washing could remove.

Mr. Townsend was a somewhat unusual clergyman. He allowed a Methodist preacher to speak from his pulpit, for which the Bishop issued an inhibition against Mr. Townsend, and he and a Justice of the Peace, Mr. Wroughton, had a disorderly scene in the church. Mr. Townsend died in 1816.

Who would have thought that the tomb of St. Osmond in Salisbury Cathedral also holds the remains of a murderer? It is said Lord Stourton, who was hanged in the Market Place of Salisbury on 16th March 1557, with a silken noose (as befitted his rank), also rests there. For 200 years a wire noose hung over the tomb, but it was removed in 1780. Yet witnesses have claimed to have seen its luminous outline within living memory.

Among documents discovered at Longleat are those which record the feud between Lord Stourton, whose estate was at Stourhead, and his steward, William Hartgill. This lasted for nearly twenty years – between 1540 and 1557. Lord Stourton, whose family had lived at Stourhead since Saxon times, accused his steward and his steward's son of diverting money to themselves, which should have passed to him. One official document reads: 'Some days after Lord Stourton had "falled utterly out" with William Hartgill, he was with a number of his retainers, local landowners, and farmers round the council table at Stourton House. His lordship finally rose and held up a glass of wine. "Gentlemen," he said, with eyes blazing, "the toast is the Hartgill family – left-handed." With enthusiasm they seized their glasses with their left hands and emptied them, indicating they drank to the Hartgill downfall . . .' Lord Stourton's invitation was clear : his steward was murdered.

Index of Place Names